SEX, LOVE & HOMOPHOBIA

Lesbian, gay, bisexual and transgender lives

Vanessa Baird

Amnesty International

Sex, Love and Homophobia
Vanessa Baird
Preface: Grayson Perry
Foreword: Archbishop Desmond Tutu

July 2004
© Amnesty International UK
99-119 Rosebery Avenue
London EC1R 4RE
From 2005, Amnesty International UK's address is:
17-25 New Inn Yard
London EC2A 3EY

www.amnesty.org.uk

The views expressed in this book do not necessarily reflect the
views of Amnesty International.

Cover photographs (featured in the book) are: Bomb blast,
London, 1999 © David Thomson/ AP (see page 35); Protest at
a gay marriage, Chicago, 1998 © Michael S Green/AP (see page
37); Rainbow flag, Brazil, 2003 © PA Photos/EPA (see page
99). Others © Marie-Anne Ventoura (also inside covers)

Design: *Cover* Rich Cowley. *Text* Deborah Gilkes
Acknowledgements: Kate Mariat for advice, support and gener-
ous help with research. Raj Rajukumar and Liz Wilkinson for
additional help

ISBN 1 873328 57 5
AIUK product code PB273

British Library Cataloguing in Publication Data.
A catalogue record for this book is available from the
British Library.

Preface

This book has strongly reminded me that when I go out wearing a dress it is not just a thrill, but a political act that in some parts of the world could get me arrested, imprisoned or even killed. My sexual orientation is not just about who or what turns me on: it goes to the very core of my identity. If I were afraid of expressing openly such a fundamental part of my personality, I would be doomed to live a half life. I did not choose my sexuality and whatever threat others perceive from me is but the product of their fear, for I only wish to celebrate all that I am.

Sex, Love and Homophobia has made me grateful to all those who have fought for acceptance in the past. It is a chilling reminder that in many countries homosexuals and the transgendered still do not enjoy the freedom to be – literally – themselves.

In 1973 I found out that my innocent habit of wearing women's clothes was a 'shocking perversion' termed transvestism when I read an article in the *News of the World*. I spent many hours poring over psychology textbooks trying to find out more about the 'unnatural' desires from which I 'suffered'. But here is a book that neither sensationalises nor pathologises the behaviour of people with a minority sexual orientation, a book that is very accessible to young people and is also a moving and serious document of the history, culture and politics of the lesbian, gay, bisexual and transgendered world of which I am proud to play a small part.

Grayson Perry, London 2004

Foreword

A student once asked me if I could have one wish granted to reverse an injustice, what would it be? I had to ask for two. One is for world leaders to forgive the debts of developing nations which hold them in such thrall. The other is for the world to end the persecution of people because of their sexual orientation, which is every bit as unjust as that crime against humanity, apartheid.

This is a matter of ordinary justice. We struggled against apartheid in South Africa, supported by people the world over, because black people were being blamed and made to suffer for something we could do nothing about – our very skins. It is the same with sexual orientation. It is a given. I could not have fought against the discrimination of apartheid and not also fight against the discrimination which homosexuals endure, even in our churches and faith groups. And I am proud that in South Africa, when we won the chance to build our own new constitution, the human rights of all have been explicitly enshrined in our laws. My hope is that one day this will be the case all over the world, and that all will have equal rights.

For me this struggle is a seamless rope. Opposing apartheid was a matter of justice. Opposing discrimination against women is a matter of justice. Opposing discrimination on the basis of sexual orientation is a matter of justice.

It is also a matter of love. Every human being is precious. We are all of us part of God's family. We must all be allowed to love each other with honour.

Yet all over the world, lesbian, gay, bisexual and transgender people are persecuted. We treat them as pariahs and push them outside our communities. We make them doubt that they too are children of God – and this must be nearly the ultimate blasphemy.

We blame them for what they are. Churches say that the expression of love in a heterosexual monogamous relationship includes the physical, the touching, embracing, kissing, the genital act – the totality of our love makes each of us grow to become increasingly godlike and compassionate. If this is so for the heterosexual, what earthly reason have we to say that it is not the case with the homosexual?

In *Sex, Love and Homophobia* you will read about those who wish to love one another as an expression of their everyday lives, just like anyone, anywhere. You will hear the voices of the persecuted and those who struggle for justice. You will also hear some of the voices of those who hate, fear and persecute. This important book brings together these voices, these diverse ends of the rainbow, because we are all one people.

Hatred and prejudice are such destructive forces. They destroy human beings, communities and whole societies – and they destroy the hater, too, from the inside. Reading the words of homophobia that are quoted in this book is frightening, it is terrifying. We all have within us a seed, a potential, that can grow into prejudice, hatred and destruction. But this book illuminates anew the bleak wasteland that is prejudice. It illuminates more clearly than ever that a loving, understanding humanity is sustained by justice.

A parent who brings up a child to be a racist damages that child, damages the community in which they live, damages our hopes for a better world. A parent who teaches a child that there is only one sexual orientation and that anything else is evil denies our humanity and their own too. We cannot answer hate with hate. We can only answer it with love, understanding and a belief in and commitment to justice.

Sex, Love and Homophobia is a bright light on the path to justice. I hope that those who read it are inspired to help build a world of human understanding, compassion and equality: a true rainbow world.

Archbishop Desmond Tutu
Cape Town, 2004

Introduction

We live in extreme times – and this is most obvious when it comes to the fraught arena of homosexuality and transgender.

Openly gay or lesbian stars and story-lines appear on our TV screens like never before. Homosexuals are closer than ever to sharing equal civil and social rights with heterosexuals.

But recent years have also witnessed an increase in the number of countries and states where homosexuality is punishable by death. Even within countries, attitudes are becoming increasingly polarised. The most obvious example is the United States. While San Francisco boasts the largest openly gay community of any city in the world, anti-homosexual movements in Kansas, Ohio and Colorado advocate as a 'Christian duty' the rejection, and in some cases even killing, of gay people.

It's probably safe to say that at no time in human history have homosexuality and transgender been so exposed to public scrutiny. On all continents today homosexuality is the subject of heated debate and controversy, not least when it is discussed in association with religious beliefs. Newspapers in regions where just a decade ago such matters were strictly taboo now bristle with exchanges and letters. Phone-in radio programmes and website chat rooms are even more popular places for discussing the issue. Homosexuality was said not to exist in most African countries not so long ago. Now it seems the air waves can't stop talking about it.

For the people at the heart of all this – gay, lesbian, bisexual or transgender individuals – the attention is a double-edged sword.

On the one hand the focus represents a tremendous opportunity to finally get the 'love that dare not speak its name' out of the shadows and into public acceptance. Hopefully this will lead to decriminalisation of homosexuality in some of the 80 or so countries where it is still illegal. It may lead to sexual minority people gaining recognition as citizens with equal rights and responsibilities.

But the spotlight comes at a cost. Lesbian and gay people who form or join organisations, be they political or social, are being violently persecuted in many parts of the world where before they might have gone unnoticed. This has been the case in Uganda, Zimbabwe, Zambia and El Salvador where such groups are relatively new. The targeting and killing of transgender people has become an epidemic on the streets of some Latin American countries: Argentina, Brazil and Venezuela have particularly worrying records. Jamaica is also witnessing a rash of homophobic beatings and murders.

The heightened awareness of homosexuality makes it harder for lesbian or gay individuals – especially teenagers – to pass unnoticed, or at least unremarked upon. Where homosexual teenagers of past decades suffered from silence, repression and the taboos surrounding the discussion of their kind, today's are perhaps more likely to suffer from explicit taunts and bullying. According to the British organisation Stonewall a survey conducted in 2000 showed that 72 per cent of young lesbians, gay men and bisexuals had either played truant or feigned illness to avoid homophobic abuse in school, while some 40 per cent had attempted suicide on at least one occasion. The impact on the education of young gay people is clear. The first school established especially for lesbian and gay teenagers opened in New York in 2003 and had no difficulty attracting students to enrol.

About the book
The purpose of this book is to give an insight into Lesbian, Gay, Bisexual and Transgender (LGBT for short) rights in the world today. The format is deliberately easy-to-read and can be dipped into according to interest. It can be read from A to Z, from Z or A – or in any order that takes your fancy.

But a snapshot of the state of things today makes little sense without the anchors of history and culture. So this book also includes what has been, up until fairly recently, the 'hidden history' of lesbian and gay people over the past couple of millennia. This underlines the fact that LGBT people have always existed, despite popular claims that homosexuality is just 'a lifestyle', and a fashionable one at that. It also shows us how periods of relative tolerance have been followed by waves of persecution and repression, amounting to genocide, in medieval Catholic Europe, Nazi Germany or Maoist China. This book examines the roots of such violence and hostility.

But perhaps more important than the overviews of history or political movements are the personal stories of people struggling just to live their lives and express their loves, without hindrance or hate. It is these personal human stories that make the most potent argument for equality and for recognition of the human rights of LGBT people.

It may seem obvious to many of us now that LGBT people have human rights. For many years the International Lesbian and Gay Association (ILGA) has campaigned for these rights on a global scale. But it is only comparatively recently that human rights organisations have taken an interest in those persecuted on the grounds of sexual orientation or gender variation.

Amnesty International led the way when, after years of internal debate, it extended its mandate to include those held captive on account of their sexuality as 'prisoners of conscience'. The Romanian sportswoman Mariana Cetiner became AI's first gay prisoner of conscience in 1995 and a letter-writing campaign by AI members across the world played a crucial role in securing her release in 1998.

Since then other human rights organisations such as the US-based Human Rights Watch and the International Gay and Lesbian Human Rights Commission have campaigned internationally and raised awareness at the United Nations.

An issue that is only just beginning to 'break silence' is that of intersex people: those born with conditions that used to be called 'hermaphroditism'. In a sense, intersex and transgender pose the most radical challenge to narrow and damaging prejudices about what is male and what is female. But the human rights of intersex people are currently being violated on a wide and routine basis.

There is still a long way to go – as the pages of this book show – but much has been achieved. More is being achieved every day. Every time an LGBT person 'comes out', or whenever a straight person challenges prejudice, hatred and inequality, humanity takes another small but significant step towards creating a fairer world.

Vanessa Baird
2004

Glossary

LGBT lesbian, gay, bisexual, and transgender.

Sexual minorities same as above.

Homosexual in theory applied to both men and women, but some women feel it refers more to men. Comes from the Greek – *homo*, same and the Latin *sexualis*, sexual. Its negative use and medical connotations have led many lesbian and gay people to reject it as a term.

Heterosexual men and women who are attracted to the opposite gender.

Gay more commonly used to describe homosexual men, but increasingly women refer to themselves as gay.

Lesbian women who are sexually attracted to other women. 'Dyke' used by some women too.

Bisexual men and women who are attracted to both sexes.

Transgender general term that can include the following: *transsexual* a person who has or is undergoing some form of gender reassignment or someone who lives in the gender identity other than their birth identity; *transvestite* someone who dresses according to the norms of the opposite gender. In the world of entertainment they are known as Drag Queens or Drag Kings; *intersexual* someone who has one of 200 or so intersex conditions, which used to be referred to as 'hermaphroditism'.

Queer originally a pejorative word used mainly to describe homosexual men, now reclaimed to cover pretty much all the above, including even gay-oriented heterosexuals.

Homophobia fear and hatred of homosexuality, but sometimes used to include transgender, more precisely known as transphobia.

Same-sex sex another way of saying homosexual sex.

Sodomy now understood to be anal sex, but was also used historically to include bestiality and female same-sex acts.

Against nature

A

'Carnal knowledge of any person against the order of nature' is an
offence which can carry a sentence of life imprisonment.
Ugandan penal code[1]

Uganda, 1999: the order went out. All suspected homosexuals – men
and women – were to be rounded up and arrested. They were then
humiliated and incarcerated. Many were physically abused. Some
were raped. Then they were sent into exile. Uganda's President
Yoweri Museveni was putting into practice his country's law that
interprets homosexuality as a crime 'against the law of nature'.[2] In the
80 or so countries that outlaw homosexuality, this is a common
formulation for anti-gay legislation.[3]

But the objection to same-sex love that the Ugandan president was
invoking has far more ancient roots than the colonial law he was
using. In the fourth century BC in Greece the philosopher Plato had
praised same-sex love in his *Symposium* and *Phaedrus*. But in his later
work, *Laws*, he condemned homosexuality on the basis that the only
legitimate purpose for sex was to bear children.[4] At the beginning of
the Christian era, the Apostle Paul drew upon Old Testament
prohibitions in his condemnation of same-sex practices:

*'God gave them unto vile affections; for even their women did
change the natural use into that which is against nature. And
likewise unto men, leaving the natural use of the woman, burned in
their lust one toward another; men with men working that which is
unseemly...'* (Romans 1:26-28)

Homo-erotic scene decorating an Athenian red-figure cup by Briseis painter. fifth century BC.

The influential theologian Augustine of Hippo, despite having had a passionate relationship with another young man in his youth, decided that sex was a weakness and homosexuality a sin. He did not mince his words: 'These foul offences which be against nature [ought to be] everywhere and at all times detested and punished, just as those of Sodom.' Augustine believed that the body of man was superior to that of a woman and for a man to use his body 'like a woman' was to defile it.[5]

Complex nature

The term 'nature', observes cultural critic Raymond Williams, is one of the most complex in the language. It is also one of the most dangerous. For centuries the idea that same-sex activity is 'unnatural' has underpinned homophobia: the fear, hatred or persecution of homosexuals. By this argument, what is not natural is monstrous. And monsters, like demons, must be slain if the 'natural order' of

'You're neither unnatural, nor abominable, nor mad; you're as much part of what people call nature as anyone else; only you're unexplained as yet – you've not got your niche in creation.'
Radclyffe Hall (1883-1943) British author of *The Well of Loneliness* 1928, which was banned for 'obscenity'.

things is to be preserved.

It is impossible to say how many millions of people who did not fit the heterosexual norm have lost their lives to this idea of 'nature'. The count must include all those burnt at the stake for sodomy during medieval and renaissance times. All those hung or drowned in later eras. All those, during the 20th century, who were worked to death in concentration camps, driven to suicide by psychiatric treatments, medical experimentation, imprisonment. All those currently being executed or 'disappeared' under various attempts to 'clean up' society or to impose religious order.

In these times of population growth and environmental destruction, to insist that sexual activities lead to procreation may seem an outdated rationale for condemning homosexuality. Contraception is widely practised around the world, while there are many forms of sex that are non-procreative yet are not condemned. Indeed, many of the sexual practices associated with homosexuality are the same as those enjoyed by heterosexuals with impunity.

Creatures great and small

It has sometimes been claimed that homosexuality is a peculiarly human 'deviation' that does not exist in the more 'wholesome' natural world of animals. Recent scientific research into the sex lives of animals challenges this view. Zoologists have identified homosexual behaviour in no fewer than 450 species of birds and animals. More intriguing examples include the discovery that killer whales devote 'a tenth of their time to homosexual activity in the summer months'.[6] In general, research on the sexual desires of animals indicates behaviour and preferences that are similar to those of humans.

Many argue, however, that science and biology are irrelevant; that nature has nothing to do with sexuality. Sexuality – be it heterosexuality or homosexuality or bisexuality – is a social thing. Like gender it is 'socially constructed' in that people are given or adopt or react against the roles and identities created by their societies. Even beliefs about what is 'natural' or 'unnatural' are products of our societies and cultures.[7]

Whichever way you look at it, life, love and desire are varied and complex. We are all unique and different from one another. We have many, varied and wonderful ways of living, loving and having consenting sex. For people whose most intimate feelings are declared to be 'against nature', what is at stake is their basic right to be themselves, to love in ways that are true and natural to them, without being hounded or persecuted. Back in 1897, Edward Carpenter, pioneering gay liberationist, said:

'I cannot regard my sexual feelings as unnatural or abnormal, since they have disclosed themselves so perfectly and naturally and spontaneously within me.'[8]

See also: Faith and fundamentalism, Homophobia, Gay gene **and** Judges

Bisexuality

'I knew my son, Robby, was different at a very early age and he always seemed to have a hard time communicating with me. He has had many behavior issues and is currently in a program for defiant youth, where he has been for the last 18 months. He is due to come home in two weeks and I received a letter yesterday informing me that he was bisexual. I must be honest... I have always been against same-sex relationships and I guess that is why Rob didn't want to tell me. I can see now that maybe a lot of his defiant behaviors were a result of keeping his feelings to himself and not being able to accept who he was...'

Debbie, a mother from urban Virginia, US, talking about her 16-year-old son.[1]

● ● ●

In Vienna, at around the turn of the 20th century, Dr Sigmund Freud was developing his ideas about childhood sexuality. The 'father of psychoanalysis' had come to the then quite revolutionary conclusion that children didn't start having sexual feelings only at puberty. Sexuality was there all along. It just changed and became more apparent at puberty. What's more, the young child was not fixed when it came to the gender of the object of their sexual feelings; she or he was effectively 'bisexual'. Later the infant would be 'conscripted' into humanity and its rigid structures of 'normal' genital heterosexuality, but for now bisexuality was the natural state.[2]

Before Freud few had thought, or dared to express, the idea that children had a sexuality – let alone that it might take the form of bisexuality.

Half a century after Freud American researcher Alfred Kinsey was also involved in work which would revolutionise the way people thought about sexuality. The project he was leading entailed conducting in-depth interviews with thousands of ordinary Americans.

During the interviews researchers Kinsey, Pomeroy and Martin found a significant number of women and men who had histories of both heterosexual and homosexual experiences and desires. From this they determined that 'the heterosexuality or homosexuality of many individuals is not an all-or-none proposition'. To deal with this they developed a classification based on the relative degrees of heterosexual or homosexual experience or desire in each person's history. Known as the Kinsey 7-point scale, it went like this:

0   Exclusively heterosexual with no homosexual
1   Predominantly heterosexual with only incidental homosexual
2   Predominantly heterosexual, but with more than incidental homosexual
3   Equally heterosexual and homosexual
4   Predominantly homosexual but more than incidental heterosexual
5   Predominantly homosexual, only incidental heterosexual
6   Exclusively homosexual with no heterosexual
x   No social-sex contacts or reactions

This offered a view which saw sexual orientation as a continuum: each person's sexual orientation falls somewhere on the scale between two extreme poles. While 10 per cent of men claimed to be exclusively gay, 37 per cent admitted to some homosexual experience and desire. These findings, published between 1948 and 1953, created a furore among moralists, physicians, clerics, law-makers, journalists and others.[3] But like Freud's discoveries, they did have a profound and lasting effect on how sexuality was viewed.

Chic and stigma

It may seem strange that more people don't openly identify as bisexual. Gay activist Carl Wittman has this answer: 'The reason so few of us are bisexual is because society made such a big stick about

● Ann Bonny and Mary 'Mark' Read, famous bisexual and cross-dressing women pirates, were brought to trial for piracy on the high seas in 1720. Sentenced to be hanged, they 'pleaded their bellies' (ie pregnancy) and were pardoned.

© The Mariners Museum, Newport News, Virginia

being homosexual that we got forced into seeing ourselves as either straight or non-straight...'

In the 1970s pop stars such as David Bowie cultivated images of androgyny and bisexuality which became quite fashionable. But Western 'bisexual chic' suffered in the 1980s from the perception that bisexuals were the route by which HIV-AIDS was crossing over from the gay into the straight community.

In one sense, the issue of bisexuality is the same as that of homosexuality: it's the homosexuality of the bisexual person that may arouse prejudice, not their heterosexuality. But bisexuals may also experienced prejudice from gay people who complain that bisexuals are avoiding the full social stigma of 'out' homosexuality. Thanks partly to the emergence of more inclusive Queer Politics, the issue of bisexuality is now less fraught; bisexuals are explicitly included and recognised within the Lesbian, Gay, Bisexual and Transgender movements around the world. And movement between gay and straight relationships and identities seems more fluid today.

See also: **Not in our culture**, **Queer** and **Youth**

C

Clitoridectomy

and other cures

'I was locked up alone in a mental institution for 72 hours with supposedly gay pornography and given drugs to make me vomit and become incontinent. There was no lavatory and no water supply in the room. They said the next part of the treatment was to apply electrodes to my genitals. After three days I begged to be let out.'

Peter Price, a gay radio broadcaster in Liverpool, UK, describing his experience of 'aversion therapy' as a teenager during the 1960s.

Peter Price had agreed to undergo treatment because his mother could not bear the idea of her 18-year-old son being homosexual. Since revealing his experiences in 1999, he has been contacted by more than 700 people to say they had received similar treatment. Many of them said they had not recovered from the trauma.

'I still get people referred to my clinic who have been told their sexuality is a disease, and we do see people who have been thoroughly messed up by attempts at treatment,' said Mike King, professor of psychiatry at the Royal Free Hospital in London in 1999.[1]

You might assume that in countries where homosexuality is now legal and enjoys a greater degree of social acceptance than ever before, such attempts to 'cure' it have become a thing of the past. Not so. As recently as 1999 John Kellet, a consultant psychiatrist at St

Cure needed? A gay man holds a placard declaring 'Homophobia is a disease', during a visit by Pope John Paul II, San Francisco 1987.

© Jacques M.Chenet/CORBIS

George's hospital, South London, used the pages of the medical journal *Trends in Urology* to describe aversion therapy he had just 'successfully' delivered to a 24-year-old soldier who wanted a 'normal' life, with wife and children. Such therapies, offered on the British National Health Service, usually involve attempts to instil loathing for gay sex.

Ex-gay movement

In the US the drive to turn homosexuals into heterosexuals has geared up in recent years with the emergence of the 'Ex-Gay Movement'.

The best known group, Exodus, has an international reach.

In 1998 a number of US groups, most of them religious and conservative, financed a nationwide campaign of full-page newspaper advertisements offering a 'cure' for homosexuality. The cure on offer is called Reparative Therapy – another term for 'conversion' therapy. The underlying assumption is that homosexuality is a kind of social and psychological sickness, the most common cause of which is family dysfunction and the failed relationships between fathers and sons and mothers and daughters.

One of the best-known organisations for carrying out reparative therapy is the National Association for Research and Therapy of Homosexuality (NARTH), a professional mental health association. Its website says:

'At risk adolescents and parents have the right to know that homosexuality is preventable and treatable and the sooner intervention takes place, the better the prognosis.'[2]

Christian groups like Coral Ridge Ministries and Focus on the Family claim that these therapies have a high cure rate. But most mental-health professional bodies are concerned about the unregulated use of these therapies and the damage they may be doing to gay people. Raymond Fowler, executive director of the American Psychology Association, says:

'Sexual orientation is not a choice and cannot be altered. Groups who try to change sexual orientation of people through so-called conversion therapy are misguided and run the risk of causing a great deal of psychological harm.'[3]

Many psychiatrists report evidence of gays and lesbians who have become seriously depressed after the failure of their therapy; some have committed suicide. 'Ex-ex-gays' too are posting their experiences on the web. Dr Rob Killian, for example, describes how his therapy included not only psychotherapy, singing hymns, and wearing tight clothes in bed, but also marrying a woman. He concludes:

'Reparative therapy does not offer wholeness. It seeks to compartmentalize the unwanted feeling into a hated part of one's being that is buried and ignored... The personal experience not only did not lead to mental or spiritual health. It gave me even more reason to hate my father and did nothing to assist me in loving my wife more... Reparative therapy is dangerous.'[4]

A history of cures

There is nothing new about people trying to 'cure' homosexuality. It has a long and bloody history.

Prior to the 19th century homosexuality was considered a sin and a crime. The solution was to get rid of the people who practised it. In suggesting that there might be a scientific cause for homosexuality, pioneers such as Karl Heinrich Ulrichs, John Addington Symonds and Havelock Ellis had hoped that greater understanding and social tolerance might ensue. To some limited extent this did happen. But the search for a scientific explanation was a double-edged sword: with it came the quest for a scientific cure. Scientists, medical professionals and others have tried to cure 'deviant' sexuality in a vast range of ways. These have included surgery, hormone treatment, aversion therapy, electric shock treatment, psychiatry, hypnotism and psycho-religious therapies.

Throughout the 20th century and on both sides of the Atlantic all manner of remedies were dreamed up. Some of the more entertainingly absurd are:

- a special diet of Brussels sprouts to protect children against becoming homosexual
- beauty therapy for lesbians
- visits to female prostitutes for gay men
- marriage in combination with study of abstract subjects such as maths.

Other therapies that gay and lesbian people have undergone are not amusing. They have amounted to extreme violations of their bodies, minds – and their human rights. Perhaps the most violent form of therapy has been surgery. Clitoridectomies and hysterectomies were performed on lesbians in the US as late as the 1950s.[5] In the USSR experiments were conducted to remove the testicles of homosexual men and replace them with those of heterosexuals. In Nazi concentration camps gay men were used extensively for experimentation.[6] In the United States until the 1950s lobotomy was favoured: cutting nerve fibres in the front of the brain eliminated homosexual drives (and most other sexual and emotional reactions).[7]

Some scientists looked for the source of homosexuality in the hormones, believing that lesbians had higher levels of the male hormone testosterone and gay men had higher levels of the female hormone oestrogen. This theory has since been disproved. Hormone therapies were developed which involved using steroids to 'butch' up gay men and 'femme out' lesbians, with little effect except that gay men experienced increased sex drive, but their orientation remained the same.

In their quest for a cure, US scientists even tried using radiation therapy on homosexuals.[8]

Shrink it

Psychiatry provided another line of attack. Perhaps the 'sickness' of homosexuality lay not in the body, but in the mind. Electro-convulsive therapy (ECT), which had been devised by Ugo Cerletti in 1938, became a common means of trying to cure homosexuals. This was used in Britain well into the 1960s. Aversion therapy was most popular: heterosexual arousal would be rewarded and homosexual attraction punished. Often this was done by using electric shocks or emetics. In Spain, under General Franco, homosexuals were placed in a 'rehabilitation' centre where they underwent such treatments.[9] During the 1970s and 1980s 'suspected' gay men and lesbians in the South African Defence Force (SADF) were forced to undergo 'conversion therapy' and other forms of treatment without their consent. This included aversion therapy and 'chemical castration', which involved drugs that suppress or remove the sex drive.[10]

Less violent, but damaging nonetheless, was the resort to psychoanalysis. In the 1950s American psychiatrist Dr Edmund Berger spoke of homosexuality as 'a kind of psychic masochism in which the unconscious sets a person on a course of self destruction'. Find the cause, a dominating mother for example, and you could find the cure.[11]

Today some in the US medical profession still see homosexuality as some kind of disorder. Most prominent is Charles Socarides, psychiatrist and author of *Homosexuality: A Freedom too Far* (1995). He sees male homosexuality as 'a neurotic adaptation' resulting from 'smothering mothers and abdicating fathers'. There are several variations on this theme. Pro-cure psychiatrists argue that they are treating those 'who want to change'; that they are acting in the patients' best interests in trying to rid them of a disorder that brings distress, discrimination and social stigma. US philosopher Edward Stein says:

'Conversion therapy is no more appropriate response to social conditions facing lesbians and gay men than bleaching the skin of

non-whites is an appropriate response to racial injustice.'[12]

The claim that homosexuals may submit voluntarily to treatment must not be taken at face value. Often lesbians and gays may be placed under considerable family pressure to visit a psychiatrist or seek a treatment. Aversion may be forced upon individuals – without local human rights organisations lifting a finger to oppose such violations. In April 2001 the National Human Rights Commission of India refused to consider a case brought before it concerning involuntary aversion therapy and other forms of psychiatric abuse aimed at homosexuals. The commission explained its decision by stating 'sexual minority rights did not fall under the purview of human rights'.[13]

Compulsory treatment and abuse

The treatment of homosexuality as a mental illness persists even in countries where homosexuality is not criminalised. In Russia police are known to have placed lesbians in psychiatric hospitals against their will solely on the grounds of sexual orientation – sometimes at the request of family members or friends. Alla Pitcherskaia, for example, alleged she had been repeatedly charged with the crime of 'hooliganism' and detained by the Russian militia because of her sexual orientation. When she visited her girlfriend who was being forcibly held in a psychiatric institution, she herself was registered as a 'suspected lesbian' and told to go to her local clinic. Instead she fled the country and claimed asylum in the US. Her application was initially rejected because the Russian authorities motive was to 'treat' or 'cure' and not to punish. This decision was later overturned.[14]

Much of the abuse of human rights of LGBT people around the world today is being carried out within the context – or behind the pretext – of 'cure'. Young lesbians are being raped and forced into marriage, especially in societies where marriage is virtually compulsory. The rape of lesbians in custody is often accompanied with the comment that this will 'cure' them of their lesbianism. And the perception of homosexuality as a disorder that needs to be 'put right' serves to legitimise such violence.

See also: Genes, Untermenschen, **and** Homophobia

D.

Diversity... and identity

'How I do begin describing myself so that anyone can understand...
My experience in England has led me to the conclusion that most
people are unable to see me whole. That is – if you're lesbian
you're white, and if you're Chinese you're exotic, passive,
inscrutable, and the whole pack of racist stereotypes... Sure, being
a lesbian is intricately woven into my web of identity. But so is the
part of me that feels alien in this country, lonely behind my wall of
defences, inarticulate in my deepest pain. These are also parts of
my inner core. So when women talk about coming out as a lesbian,
I want to ask – can I come out as a person first?'
Yik Hui[1]

In Thailand lady boys, or *kathoey*, dress as women and are very much
a part of street and city life. They may or may not be gay.[2] In Surinam,
women who call each other *mati* have long-term intense, often open,
relationships with each other in between or alongside their sexual
relationship with men. But they don't think of themselves as
'lesbian'.[3] Among men in Latin America a distinction is often made
between the 'insertive partner' and the 'receptive' partner. Only the
latter is considered truly homosexual – a *marecon*. Female terms like
loca or *bicha* are used for receptive gay males.[4] In Indonesia and the
Philippines women called *tombois* dress as men and are referred to as

An Israeli woman, covering her face with traditional Arab keffiyeh, takes part in a demonstration against the Israeli occupation of the West Bank and Gaza Strip, during the annual gay love parade in Tel Aviv. Tens of thousands of Israeli LGBT people participated in the parade. June 2002.

© EPA/Sven Nackstrand

'he'. Their more feminine partners do not earn this title and may even be considered heterosexual in spite of the fact that they are involved in a same-sex relationship.[5] And in China the most popular word for a lesbian, gay or bisexual person is *tongzhi*, meaning comrade. In the course of conducting 200 interviews, researcher Chou Wha-shan found that not one *tongzhi* referred to himself or herself as *tongxinglina* – a homosexual.[6]

'We are everywhere' is the traditional rallying cry of the lesbian and gay liberation movement. It may be true that sexual minority people may be found in all corners of the world. But that does not mean that there is such a thing as a universal gay or transgender identity. For many people in the world the idea of a fixed sexual identity is somewhat alien. Traditional Chinese culture, for example, has a more fluid conception of sexuality and treats homosexuality as an option that most people can experience rather than something restricted to a sexual minority having fixed, inherent traits.[7]

Today 'diversity' is the salient characteristic of sexual minorities and their political movements worldwide. Diversity can be found in the way in which people may perceive themselves, their sexuality and other types of identity, shaped as they are by specific cultures and traditions. But diversity can also be found within movements. This is reflected in the now common acronym of LGBT – the Lesbian, Gay, Bisexual and Transgender movement. It was not always this way.

I am what I am

And what I am

Needs no excuses.

I deal my own deck,

Sometimes the ace

Sometimes the deuces.

And there's no return and no deposit,

So it's time to open up your closet!

Life's not worth a damn,

'Till you can say, 'Hey, world,

I am what I am!'

Singer Gloria Gaynor, *I Am What I Am*

In the early days of Gay Lib, the movement was anything but diverse. It was predominantly white, western, male and middle-class. The flowering of the black civil rights and the women's movements in the 1960s and 1970s challenged this. Some black and Asian lesbians formed separate groups, feeling that a false universalism was being promoted that did not reflect their reality. In the 1970s groups such as the national Black Feminist Organisation were formed and the first Black Lesbian Conference was held in San Francisco in 1980.

The same issues emerged in relation to class, with working-class lesbians and gays feeling that the movement reflected a middle-class reality. Bisexuals and transgender people felt similarly sidelined. For many years the lesbian and gay movement saw transgender as completely separate. Some argued that transsexualism was a product of stereotypical ways of thinking. If, for example, a man could be more feminine, perhaps it would not be necessary for him to alter his gender. Others believed that transgendered people had been misled and exploited by the medical profession. More hostile reactions came from some feminists – both gay and straight – who felt that male-to-female transsexuals, having been brought up male, could never know what it was like to be female. In her book *Transsexual Empire*, US academic Janice Raymond argued that transsexuals were the insidious tools of the patriarchal system, infiltrating women's circles and dividing women.[8]

However, the more inclusive politics of the 1990s led to new alliances and coalitions, some of which have been helpful to transgender people. In Argentina, Brazil and Colombia, for example, the raising of transgender issues by LGBT groups has led to changes in law and far greater awareness of human rights violations. Influential sections of the women's movement have also changed their position on transgender.

See also: Vegetarian sisterhoods, Trans Liberation **and Out**

E

Equality

'My darling it means sweet motherfucking nothing at all. You can rape me, rob me, what am I going to do if you attack me? Wave the Constitution in your face? I'm just a nobody black queen... But you know what? Ever since I heard about that Constitution, I feel free inside.'

Drag-queen in Johannesburg, on the inclusion of an anti-discrimination on the grounds of sexual orientation clause in South Africa's Constitution.[1]

In 1948 the newly formed United Nations (UN) drew up and adopted the Universal Declaration of Human Rights (UDHR) in response to the atrocities committed during the Second World War.

Recognising the fact that people had been tortured and killed by the Nazis because of their identity or beliefs, key provisions were included to outlaw discrimination on such grounds as race, sex, religion or political opinion.

Although gay men and lesbians were targeted by the Nazis and were among the millions sent to their deaths in concentration camps, the discrimination clauses of the Universal Declaration did not explicitly recognise abuses based on sexual orientation. The suffering of lesbians and gay men remained untold.

For more than 50 years the abuses faced by gay, lesbian bisexual and transgender people around the world continued to be surrounded by silence and indifference. The comprehensive body of international human rights standards developed since the Universal Declaration of

Army Colonel Margarethe Cammermeyer, a 26-year service member and decorated Vietnam veteran, was discharged from the Washington State Army National Guard for being a lesbian. Cammermeyer, one of the highest-ranking officers ever to be discharged for homosexuality, revealed her orientation under questioning in 1989.

© FrishPhoto Inc

Human Rights did not contain a single reference to sexual orientation or gender identity.

Tabling – and derailing – equality

In spring 2003 the UN Commission on Human Rights began discussing a draft resolution entitled 'Human Rights and Sexual Orientation'. This, for the first time in the UN's history, called upon 'all states to promote and protect the human rights of all persons regardless of their sexual orientation'. Proposed by Brazil, it was seconded by South Africa and backed by more than 19 countries. Campaigning for the resolution Amnesty International said:

'Its adoption is the only way to end the intolerable exclusion of lesbian gay, bisexual and transgender people from the full protection of the UN system ... Governments who vote against it will be signalling that they no longer believe in the fundamental premise of the Universal Declaration of Human Rights: that all human beings are equal in dignity and rights, without distinction of any kind.'[2]

But equality was not to be. The vote was derailed by an alliance of five Muslim countries – Pakistan, Egypt, Libya, Saudi Arabia and Malaysia – who introduced amendments designed to kill it off. They were backed by the Vatican. These amendments removed all references to discrimination on the basis of sexual orientation and rendered the resolution meaningless.[3] In some 80 countries homosexuality is still illegal and in nine states it is punishable by death.[4]

Although the UN resolution did not succeed it highlighted an issue that some try their best to keep in the dark. Many governments at the UN have contested any attempt to address the human rights of lesbian, gay, bisexual and transgender people. Time and again, at various UN forums, governments have systematically written out references to sexual orientation and gender identity from any human rights texts being proposed. Human rights defenders working on issues of sexuality have faced vilification and exclusion. But at the same time violations based on sexual orientation and gender identity have been increasingly documented by experts appointed by the UN's Commission on Human Rights. Millions around the world face imprisonment, torture, violence and discrimination simply because of their sexual orientation or gender identity.[5]

Don't ask, don't tell

One of the areas where lesbian gay and trangender people have been most unequally treated has been within the armed forces. Even those decorated for bravery in war can be interrogated, shamed and hounded out of their jobs.

Gays and lesbians were routinely dismissed from the British armed forces until 2000, when the European Court of Human Rights ruled that they could not be banned from serving. The court found in

Violations of human rights: some examples

Equal right to life
People convicted of homosexual sex can be executed by law in Afghanistan, Sudan, Iran, Mauritania, Saudi Arabia and Yemen. This was the fate of Ali Sharifi, hanged in Iran for having gay sex. Two young men in Afghanistan, Abdul Sami, aged 18, and Bismillah, 22, accused of sodomy, were crushed to death.[6]

Equal freedom from torture and ill-treatment
Police forced two Malaysian men, Munawar Anees and Sukma Darmawan, to confess under torture to having sex with former Deputy Prime Minister, Anwar Ibrahim.[7]

Equal freedom from arbitrary detention
Five lesbian and gay friends in Uganda were arrested, tortured and forced to flee their country.[8] 'Fatima', a 16-year old gay Zimbabwean man, was arrested for wearing a bandanna on his head. Police put him in a cell with six other prisoners who were told: 'Here's a homosexual. You can do whatever you want with him.'[9]

Equal freedom of expression and association
Mirsad, a Lebanese website, was shut down and its editor prosecuted after hosting information on gay and lesbian issues. A Hungarian LGBT youth group was banned by the authorities because it admitted young people under the age of 19 and was thus considered to be encouraging child abuse.[10]

Equal social and economic rights
Few states provide protection against discrimination for lesbian and gay people in areas such as employment, housing, parenting and health care. Only a handful of states, including Denmark and the Netherlands, give full and equal recognition to same-sex partnerships.

'I don't believe they [homosexuals] should have any rights at all.'
President Robert Mugabe of Zimbabwe.[11]

'All human beings are born free and equal in dignity and rights'
Article 1, Universal Declaration of Human Rights.

favour of four gay enlistees who had been dismissed from the military and labelled the ban 'a grave interference in private lives'.

In the United States, Joe Zuniga was 'Soldier of Year' in 1992, honoured for his bravery in Operation Desert Storm. He came out as gay in 1993 and was dismissed a month later.

Army Pfc Shannon Emery, stationed in South Korea, told her commanding officer that drunken US soldiers had tried to rape her. The commanding officer dismissed the charge and the men she had reported then accused Emery of being a lesbian. An investigation into Emery's sexual orientation was begun and she was encouraged to name women who might be gay in return for lenient treatment. Army officials eventually dropped court-martial and discharge proceedings owing to lack of evidence.[12]

The hounding of lesbians and gays in the US armed forces effectively continues, despite President Bill Clinton's 1993 'compromise' policy of 'Don't Ask, Don't Tell'. This allows lesbians and gay men to serve in the forces provided that they do not disclose their sexuality. It has not worked. Rather than ensuring that the forces kept their lesbian and gay staff, discharges and harassment have increased. In 1999 there were 1,034 discharges of lesbian and gay staff – a 73 per cent increase from before Clinton's policy was announced. There were 968 incidents of harassment of gay and lesbian staff during 1999, ranging from taunts to the murder of Pfc Barry Winchell at Fort Campbell, Kentucky. Women in particular have been targeted. In 1996, 29 per cent of all personnel discharged for homosexuality were women, although women made up only 13 per cent of the overall forces. It is not uncommon for women who report sexual harassment or assault to be accused of being gay in retaliation. The threat of war in Iraq contributed to a reduction in dismissals of gay soldiers in 2002, though 24 linguists, most trained in Arabic and Korean, were sacked because of their sexual orientation.[13]

Progress

In recent years lesbian and gay rights issues have made their way on to the human rights agenda. This progress is chiefly attributable to the courage, dynamism and increased visibility of activists. Some significant victories have been won, bringing about legal reforms and changes in cultural attitudes.

In 1996 South Africa became the first country in the world to prohibit discrimination on the grounds of sexual orientation in its constitution. Ecuador followed suit. Progressive local authorities in Brazil, Canada, Mexico, Argentina and a number of Western European countries have passed other anti-discrimination and anti-vilification laws. In Australia transgender people have specific legal protection from discrimination. In the 43 states of the Council of Europe cases of discrimination against sexual minorities can be challenged under the European Convention of Human Rights. The European Union Charter of Fundamental Rights, passed in 2000, prohibits discrimination on the grounds of sexual orientation.

See also **Judges, Faith, Homophobia, Rainbow and** Zapatistas

F.

Faith and fundamentalism

'Homosexuality makes God vomit'
Jay Grimstead, US Evangelical Christian activist.[1]

● ● ●

Abhorrence of homosexuality crops up in many faiths around the world. Religion is often invoked as a reason for condemning and persecuting people who share sexual intimacy with their own sex or bend the gender rules in some way.

Buddhism

Of the world's major religions Buddhism appears to be most positive towards homosexuality. The Jataka tales of early Buddhism, which originated in India, celebrate the Buddha's loving relationship with his disciple Anand. In one tale they are described as two deer, always together, cuddling, muzzle to muzzle. In another they are two young men who refuse to marry so that they can remain together.

The Chinese Buddhist tradition has tales of lesbian and transgender behaviour among nuns. A Buddhist nun founded the Ten Sisters Society which resisted heterosexual marriage and held ceremonies of same-sex unions up until the 19th century. Meanwhile, Christian missionaries visiting Japan in the 16th century were appalled to find same-sex relationships quite common and accepted within Buddhist monasteries. A visitor to pre-invasion Tibet, Heinrich Harrer, reported that same-sex intimacy was common in monasteries there too.[2] In Thailand in 2003 there were reports of a row over homosexuality in Buddhist monasteries: one side arguing

Anti-gay protesters outside the Broadway United Methodist Church, Chicago, where a marriage between two gay men had taken place. November 1998.

© AP Photo/Michael S Green

that monks have been corrupted by 'rich gay men' and 'foreigners', the other making the case for a tolerant attitude towards sexual orientation.[3] Today there are a number of Gay Buddhist organisations and HIV-AIDS projects in the West.

Hinduism

Modern Hinduism appears hostile to homosexuality. Members of the growing traditionalist Shiv Sena movement hold the view that homosexuality is un-Hindu, un-Indian and has no place within the history, religion and traditions of the subcontinent.

But there are other traditions associated with Hinduism that are more positive. The Tantric tradition, according to researcher Mina Kumar, provides 'a religiously sanctioned role for lesbians'. The female organ is seen as the sole seat of all happiness.

Transgender *hijras* or eunuchs consider themselves to belong to a separate Hindu-related religious sect devoted to the Mother Goddess Bahuchara Mata. Arjuna, one of the heroes of the epic poem Mahaharata, is claimed by contemporary *hijras* as one of their mythic forbears.[4]

Islam

The only actual reference to homosexuality in the Qur'an can be found in the sections about Sodom and Gomorrah. People engaging in homosexual acts are referred to as the 'the people of Lot'. The prophet Mohammed is believed to have said:

'Doomed by God is he who does what Lot's people did... No man should look at the private parts of another man, and no woman should look at the private parts of another woman.'[5]

For some people this is a clear condemnation of homosexuality. Others, though, have argued that the people of Sodom were punished for doing everything excessively.[6]

In Sufism, the mystic tradition of Islam, transgender and same-sex behaviour is recorded. The Sufis suffered heavily at the hands of other practitioners of Islam. One Islamic text refers to the Sufis as 'a community of Sodomites'. Punishment for homosexuality included stoning and burning. According to 12th century scholar Ibn' Abbas 'the sodomite should be thrown upside down from the highest building in town, then stoned.'[7]

Since the 1970s the situation has become difficult and dangerous for gay and transgendered people living in countries dominated by Islamic fundamentalism. The states that currently carry the death penalty for homosexuality are all Muslim-dominated, with hard-line tendencies. Even in non-Muslim countries violent stances have been taken. Sheikh Sharkhawy of the Regent's Park Mosque in London has publicly advocated the execution of gay males over the age of 10 and life imprisonment for lesbians.[8]

But there are attempts within Islam to soften attitudes. Some Muslim writers and theologians, such as Shaid Dossani and Kalid

Duran, are working to change male and homophobic interpretation of the Qur'an. Syrian-born gay activist Omar Nahas, currently living in the Netherlands, is trying to change attitudes by talking to imams (Muslim priests) about homosexuality. He says:

'Homosexuality is a sensitive subject among Muslims. Only with a great deal of patience, respect and careful choice of words can you get people to talk about it.'[9]

Judaism

The Old Testament puts it plainly:

'You shall not lie with a male as with a woman; it is an abomination... If a man lies with a male as with a woman, both of them have committed an abomination; they shall be put to death, their blood is upon them.' (Leviticus 18:22, 20:13)

'A woman shall not wear anything that pertains of man, nor shall a man put on a woman's garment; for whoever does these things is an abomination to the Lord your God.' (Deuteronomy 22:5)

Biblical scholars suggest that the harshness of these commandments may be rooted in the efforts of the ancient Israelites to distinguish themselves from the Canaanites who had inhabited the land prior to their arrival. Goddess worship was practised in the Canaanite religion and its practices included both gender and sexual variance in the form of the *quedeshim* – priests and priestesses who were 'sacred prostitutes'.

In the second century rabbinical text the *Mishna*, sexual intercourse between men is punishable by stoning. This tradition continued into the Middle Ages. Several beliefs gained strength, including the idea that men who had sex with each other would be divinely punished by early death.[10] Yet esoteric and folk traditions of Judaism that emerged in the Middle Ages appear more tolerant, mirrored by the dramatic rise of male homoerotic poetry among the Jewish poets of Spain.

Since the 1970s many gay-centred Jewish groups have been founded, including the World Congress of Gay and Lesbian Jewish Organisations. Openly gay rabbis, such as the popular British broadcaster Lionel Blue, have also had an important role to play. And transgendered Jewish singer Dana International caused a stir – and raised the profile of LGBT rights – when she won the 1997 Eurovision Song Contest to the dismay of right-wing orthodox rabbis such as Shlomo Benizri who declared: 'I feel shamed... Now we send darkness to the world.'[11]

Christianity

Some years ago a text was produced with the title *What Jesus Said About Homosexuality*. It contained blank pages. Prepared to comment on a whole range of moral and social issues, Jesus of Nazareth, it seems, had nothing to say about homosexuality.[12] Where Jesus was silent, the Apostle Paul was not and his words have been widely used to condemn homosexuality.

Around the year 1000, the western Church began to centralise power around the Pope. Heretics and those whose sexual practices were deemed contrary to the dictates of moral law, began to be classified and persecuted. Accusations of sodomy were used against political enemies. Intolerance grew through the Middle Ages and men and women accused of the crime 'so hideous it could not be named' were usually burned at the stake. Thousands more were executed under the Catholic Inquisitions of the 16th and 17th centuries and in Protestant Europe too. The Plymouth Colony of Puritans in North America, fearing that their 'new Jerusalem' might become a 'new Sodom', made sodomy punishable by death in 1636.[13]

In 1955 new discussions began when Derek Sherwin Bailey published a ground-breaking book *Homosexuality and the Western Tradition,* causing Christian writers and religious leaders to re-examine the Bible. Gay and lesbian Christians began to organise, some trying to change attitudes within their churches, others setting up new specifically gay-centred churches. In 1989 US Bishop John Selby Spong presented a re-interpretation of the biblical story of Sodom in his book *Living in Sin*. He argued that the main point of the story was not homosexuality but the violation of Middle Eastern principles of hospitality.

There has been a violent backlash from some Protestant evangelical Christians, especially in the United States. In 1990 Scriptures in America published a booklet entitled *Death Penalty for Homosexuals is Prescribed in the Bible*, which argued that Christians who do not do violence to gays are not fulfilling their responsibilities as Christians. The state in which the booklet was published, Colorado, subsequently witnessed a substantial rise in hate crimes.[14]

The Catholic Church has also adopted a more aggressive stance in recent years. In 2003 Pope John Paul II issued a special instruction condemning homosexuality, describing support for gay marriage as 'legitimising evil' and accusing gay parents of doing 'violence' to their children.

Ordination of openly gay clergy is another contentious issue, with liberals arguing for acceptance on one side and traditionalists, who rely on a literal reading of the Bible, resisting from the other. In July 2003 British Canon Jeffrey John, an openly gay (but celibate) priest was forced to withdraw from taking up his post as Anglican Bishop of Reading, amid fears that it would lead to an irreparable split in the Church. In the US, however, history was made in August 2003 when Canon Gene Robinson was appointed the Anglican Church's first openly gay bishop. Outraged traditionalists, both in the North and the global South, once again threatened schism.

Some of the other smaller Christian churches have had less trouble: the United Church of Canada has an explicit policy of welcoming gay and lesbian clergy and the Quakers have for many years conducted blessings of long-term gay and lesbian relationships.

Defending human rights with humour

Many are trying to work across faiths and cultures to defend the human rights of sexual minority people. Some have found humour to be the best tool. Dr Laura Schlesinger is a US broadcaster who dispenses advice to people who call her radio show. On one of her shows she said that, as an observant Orthodox Jew, she held that homosexuality was an abomination according to Leviticus 18:22 and she could not condone it in any way.

The following is an open letter to Dr Laura from a US citizen which was posted on the internet:

‘Dear Dr Laura

Thank you for doing so much to educate people regarding God's law. I have learned a great deal from your show, and I try to share that knowledge with as many people as I can. When someone tries to defend the homosexual lifestyle, for example, I simply remind them that Leviticus 18:22 clearly states it to be an abomination. End of debate. I do need some advice from you, however, regarding some of the specific laws and how to follow them.

a) When I burn a bull on the altar of sacrifice, I know it creates a pleasing odour for the Lord (Lev. 1:9). The problem is my neighbours. They claim the odour is not pleasing to them. Should I smite them?

b) I would like to sell my daughter into slavery, as sanctioned in Exodus 21:7. In this day and age, what do you think would be a fair price for her?

c) I know that I am allowed no contact with a woman while she is in her period of menstrual uncleanliness. (Lev. 15:19-24) The problem is, how do I tell? I have tried asking, but most women take offence.

d) Lev. 25-44 states that I may indeed possess slaves, both male and female providing they are purchased from neighbouring nations. A friend of mine claims that this applies to Mexicans but not Canadians. Can you clarify? Why can't I own Canadians?

e) I have a neighbour who insists on working on the Sabbath, Exodus 35:2 clearly states he should be put to death. Am I morally obligated to kill him myself?

f) A friend of mine feels that even though eating shellfish is an abomination (Lev 11: 10) it is a lesser abomination than homosexuality. I don't agree. Can you settle this?

g) Lev. 21:20 states that I may not approach the altar of God if I have a defect in my sight. I have to admit I wear reading glasses. Does my vision have to be 20/20, or is there some wiggle room here?

h) Most of my male friends get their hair trimmed, including hair around their temples, even though this is expressly forbidden by Lev. 19:27. How should they die?

i) I know from Lev 11:6-8 that touching the skin of a dead pig makes me unclean, but may I still play football if I wear gloves?

j) My uncle has a farm. He violates Lev. 19:19 by planting two different crops in the same field, as does his wife by wearing garments made of two different kinds of thread (cotton /polyester blend). He also tends to curse and blaspheme a lot. Is it really necessary that we go to all the trouble of getting the whole town together to stone them? (Lev. 24: 10-16) Couldn't we just bring them to death at a private family affair like we do with people who sleep with their in-laws? (Lev. 20:14)

I know you have studied these things extensively, so I am confident you can help. Thank you again for reminding us that God's word is eternal and unchanging

Your faithful listener'

See also: Homophobia **and** Vegetarian sisterhoods

G

Gay gene
and other scientific adventures

'My mother made me a homosexual.'

'If I send her the wool will she make me one too?'

Graffiti, New York

'It doesn't come from my side of family!' How many parents of a gay son or lesbian daughter have said this?

In the early 1990s a biologist called Dean Hamer, working at the US National Cancer Institute, looked into whether colloquial claims such as this have any basis in scientific truth. He placed an advertisement in a Baltimore newspaper under the headline, 'Gay Men – Do you have a Gay Brother?'[1] His work was part of a large and increasingly politicised quest for a scientific source of homosexuality. The focus in modern times has been on two areas. One, searching for a source in the genes and identifying a so-called 'gay gene'. Two, searching for a source in a brain – the so called 'gay brain'. Both have received much publicity and stoked fierce controversy.

The gay gene – or Xq28

The idea that homosexuality might be hereditary is not new. Medieval Muslim scientific writer Qusta ibn Luqa believed this was often the case. Some sexologists of the late 19th and early 20th centuries also held this view.[2] However, it took new impetus in the early 1990s with Hamer's research. Hamer isolated what he took to be a pattern of

ABORTION OF
GAY FETUSES

GENE
THERAPY

" AT LAST, DR. HAMER... THE SECRET
OF THE GAY GENE ! "

Cartoon appearing in *The Washington Blade*, 1993.

© David Brady/The Washington Blade

maternal-linked inheritance in the families of gay men and then
carried out a genetic link study to determine the location on the
female X Chromosome of the gene responsible for the pattern. His
most significant result was an increased rate of homosexuality on the
maternal side of gay men's families.

Commentators have expressed concern about this result and its
significance. Some have said that the different rate of homosexuality
among maternal and paternal relatives is not statistically significant
and questioned the base rate of homosexuality within the general

population that he used.

In 1993 and 1995 Hamer pinpointed a specific genetic marker on the X chromosome linked to homosexuality in men. He found that in 40 pairs of gay brothers, 33 had the same set of DNA sequences on the region of the chromosome called Xq28. This study was immediately used by gay activists who were hoping that the discovery of a gay gene would strengthen their cases against discrimination. However, when Ontario neurologist George Rice tried to replicate these findings he could not. He didn't discount a genetic link for homosexuality – but he didn't think Xq28 was the spot.

Groups opposing gay rights latched onto Rice's findings, saying it confirmed what they has been saying all along: that there is no gay gene, that homosexuality is a 'lifestyle' choice that deserves no legal protection. In the words of Yvette Cantu, policy analyst for the Family Research Council in the US: 'We're saying you can't grant someone minority status for something that's just a sexual behaviour, a choice.'[3]

The gay brain: it's that hypothalamus

Another theory is that the difference between homosexuals and heterosexuals lies in the brain and significant recent research has concentrated in this area.

In 1991 Simon Le Vay, a neuro-anatomist at the US Salk Institute, published a study of the size of particular cell groups in the hypothalamus – a region of the brain slightly smaller than a golf ball.[4] The hypothalamus plays a key role in sex, diet, cardiovascular performance, control of body temperature, stress, emotional response, growth and other functions. Le Vay examined 41 brains, 19 of gay men who had died of AIDs, six of straight women, and 16 of men presumed heterosexual. He found that the part of the hypothalamus known as INAH-3 was smaller in gay men than in men presumed to be heterosexual and about the same size as those of women. This suggests that gay men's INAH-3 was 'feminised'. Le Vay claimed that the study opened the door to finding the answer to the question 'what makes people gay or straight'.

His theory has been challenged, however. The fact that all the male subjects with smaller INAH-3 s had died of AIDS and that at the time of death all had decreased testosterone levels as side effect of treatments was seen as problematic. Also, no brains of lesbians were included which, if the theory were correct, should show a larger INAH-3.

Where will it all lead?

Scientific investigation into sexual orientation is fascinating and provides a rich field of work for researchers. But what is the point of such research? For the average lesbian, gay man or bisexual, it may have little relevance. The chances are that sexual orientation has multiple origins. Some theories work better for some people than others.

There are considerable risks attached to scientific research into sexuality. Might gene therapy, for example, lead to renewed attempts to 'cure' homosexuality? Could prenatal tests to detect the gene in the womb be used to abort gay foetuses? Or might prenatal therapy be used on babies in the womb to turn the gay ones straight?

In the absence of full human rights and social equality, medical science continues to be a dangerously double-edged sword for sexual minority people, with the whiff of eugenics never far away.

Most gay rights groups agree that the origins of sexuality should make no difference to people's civil, political and human rights. Equality does not require scientific justification.

See also: **Against nature, Clitoridectomy and We are family**

Homophobia
and its roots

'Homosexuality is a crime against humanity.'
Dr Paul Cameron of the Family Research Council[1]

● ● ●

Three young men get chatting in a bar called the Fireside Lounge. They are in their early 20s. Two of them know each other. The third, a student called Matthew Shepard, has not met the others before. He is gay and he imagines that they are too. A few hours later Matthew is dying, his skull shattered, bruises to his groin and inner thighs, his body tied to a fence.

The reason one of his young killers gave for beating the student to death with a pistol was that the Matthew had flirted with him. The townspeople who protested at Matthew Shepard's funeral in Casper, Wyoming supported the killers, Aaron McKinney and Russell Henderson. They carried placards saying 'God hates fags' and 'Matt in hell'.[2]

Such incidences are not just a peculiarity of small-town, Bible-belt America. Homophobic violence can erupt in even the most seemingly tolerant of places. On a warm spring evening in 1999 nailbomber David Copeland placed a lethal device in the packed Admiral Duncan pub, a well-known gay meeting place in Soho, London. The explosion killed three and caused scores of horrific injuries. The following day the LGBT organisation Stonewall received more homophobic phone calls in a few hours than it had received in the previous six months. One caller said: 'They should have got the lot of you!'[3]

It is impossible, given under-reporting due to taboos surrounding homosexuality, to give an accurate figure of the number of homophobic murders that take place around the world. Few cases ever get to trial: in Brazil only five per cent of an average 90 or so killings of LGBT people a year are tried.[4]

'Yeh man! That's how we do it in Jamaica! We take the battyman queers and burn them!'
Barman quoted by Rikki Beadle Blair, BBC Radio 4.[5]

'Not only is homosexuality a sin, but anyone who supports fags is just as guilty as they are. You are both worthy of death.'
Rev Fred Phelps, Westboro Baptist Church, Topeka, Kansas[6]

'Those who practice homosexuality embrace a culture of death. They risk their lives as well as their mental and spiritual well-being... a band of radical activists, many of them highly placed, put the well being of all society at risk to satisfy their craving for approval.'
People for the American Way of Life in 'Hostile Climate' 1998.[7]

'My father's an irritating, perverted homophobe who I'd never discuss any of it with anyway, despite him knowing.'
Jack, bisexual, transgendered British teenager, 2003.[8]

The roots of hate

In 1972 US writer George Weinberg was one of the first to coin the expression 'homophobia', defining it as 'the dread of being at close quarters with homosexuals'. Mark Freedman later described it as 'an extreme rage and fear reaction to homosexuals'. Poet Audre Lorde's 1978 definition offered more complexity: 'Fear of feelings of love for members of one's own sex and therefore hatred of those feelings in others'.[9]

But what is the basis of this fear? Many argue that it has to do with the perception that homosexuality disrupts the sexual and gender order according to so-called natural law. It's unruly – or, in the words of Pope John Paul II, 'disorderly'. Homosexuals are perceived as 'different' in ways that arouse fear or discomfort. Perhaps homosexuality taps into primal anxieties about the continuity of the race or tribe or genes. The non-procreative nature of same-sex sex

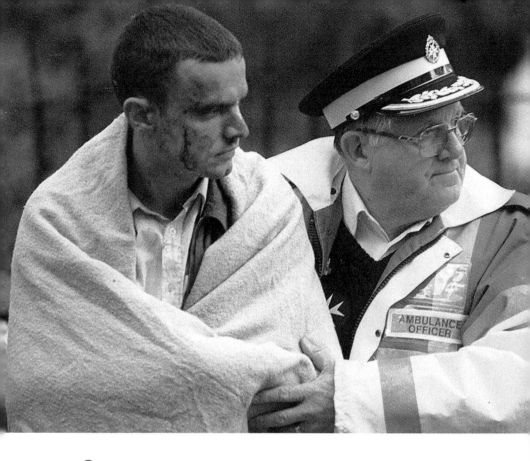

Rescue worker helps a casualty of a nailbomb that ripped through the Admiral Duncan pub, a gay meeting place in Soho, London. 30 April 1999.

(like masturbation) may be seen as wasteful and thus undesirable.

But homophobia is still a bit of a conundrum, whose roots appear complex and shifting. As historians have noted, objections to homosexuality have a capacity to mutate according to the dominant issues of the day. At times of moral panic homosexuality has been deemed 'sinful' and 'unnatural'. At times of plague, 'pestilent' and 'sick'. At times of war, 'degenerate' and even 'unpatriotic'.

In his history of the prejudice, *Homophobia*, Byrne Fone details the many things sodomy has been blamed for – including earthquakes and eclipses. Sodomites have been charged with threatening the family, the State, the natural order and the very survival of the human race. The anti-gay backlash at the outbreak of the AIDS epidemic was part of a long tradition.

Homophobia is often hitched up to other prejudices – racism or xenophobia, for example. And hostile reactions to gay men may also be connected with sexist attitudes towards women. If men are generally contemptuous of women because they believe them to be weak, irrational or inferior, they may also be contemptuous of men who (in their view) behave 'like women'.

Is it personal, psychological?

At the most basic level most of us have been conditioned, to some degree, to be homophobic. This can be challenged by creating environments and cultures that confront and actively reject the prejudice. But often homophobia runs deep and can be potent and complex at a personal level.

Of the various psychological theories that try to explain what makes an individual especially homophobic, most common is the suggestion that he or she is suppressing their own latent homosexuality. Homophobia does tend to be most visible in tight-knit macho units of men where homo-eroticism is very much in the air but homosexuality strictly forbidden and severely punished. These men may feel the need to deny any sexual component to their bonding and increase their solidarity by turning violently on 'fags' or 'queers'. This phenomenon is found especially amongst teenage gangs, police and soldiers. By attacking a gay person the individual attempts to make a clear distinction between himself (or herself) and the dreaded sexuality.[10]

But reasons for gay-bashing can also be quite simple. A study of youths who violently attacked gays in San Francisco noted that they did so because they loved the thrill and 'doing it together'. Some said they did not have anything particular against gays – they were just easy targets. They also, crucially, felt they could get away with it. Beating up 'fags' would not result in social disapproval in the way that bashing women or members of ethnic minorities might.[11]

Anti-gay sentiments may also just be fashionable. The lyrics of popular hip-hop artist Eminem are redolent with homophobia, yet many of his fans claim that they don't believe that he's really anti-gay. He's a provocateur, they say, someone who's just throwing words out there to rile us and make a statement about censorship.

'You faggots keep eggin' me on
'til I have you at knifepoint, then you beg me to stop? ...

48

My words are like a dagger with a jagged edge
That'll stab you in the head whether you're a fag or lez
Or the homosex, hermaph or a trans-a-vest.'
Eminem, 'The Marshall Mathers LP'

Even gay magazine *The Advocate* ran an admiring review which argued that people who are offended are taking it all too literally: Eminem is giving us a portrayal of homophobic thinking rather than actually advocating it himself. When asked by MTV's Kurt Loder why he wrote homophobic lyrics the musician replied: '*Faggot* to me doesn't necessarily mean gay people. *Faggot* to me just means... taking away your manhood. You're a sissy. You're a coward... You're being an asshole, or whatever...'[12]

Michael Bisogno, an 18-year-old gay youth activist who lives in Teaneck, New Jersey is not reassured:

'*A lot of the gay kids love him because he's hot. He uses the word "faggot" extensively, but some people are saying he's not homophobic, that he doesn't mean it that way. It scares me that we're looking at this and accepting it. It's a socially acceptable prejudice.*'[13]

Some counsellors who work with gay and lesbian teenagers hold that anti-gay sentiment in youth culture reflects a desire to be liked and to fit in rather than anti-gay feeling. Others see a more causal relationship. 'Those kind of lyrics incite violence against gay and lesbian people,' Dr Joyce Hunter, a research scientist at Columbia University Medical Center told *Rolling Stone*: 'It encourages young boys in schools to harass them. People say they can sing these lyrics and it doesn't mean anything. It means something.'[14]

In Jamaica some musicians actively promote homophobia. At a January 2004 gig in St Elizabeth, performers including Capleton and Sizzla sang almost exclusively about gay men, urging their audience of around 30,000 to: 'kill dem, battybwoys haffi dead, gun shots pon dem ... who want to see dem dead put up his hand' (kill them, gay men have got to die, gun shots in their head, whoever wants to see them dead, put up your hand).[15]

Is it political?

While it might be true to say that traditionalists are more likely to be politically conservative and less likely to be open to the notion of LGBT rights, the history of the 20th century warns us against making rash generalisations.

Nazi Germany and fascist Spain persecuted and executed thousands of gay people. But so did communist China. After the 1949 Maoist revolution gays were rounded up and shot. Lesbians belonging to women-only sisterhoods fled into exile. Homosexuality was declared non-existent.

Capitalist America and communist Russia may have been poles apart on ideology, but when it came to their treatment of sexual minorities they had much in common. Both subjected their lesbian and gay citizens to imprisonment and enforced medical treatment. While Stalinist Russia put homosexuality on a par with banditry, counter-revolutionary activities, espionage and sabotage, McCarthyites in the US ensured that more than 600 'sexual perverts' were purged from their government jobs on the grounds that they posed a threat to national security.[16]

In Latin America from the 1960s to the 1980s a similar mirroring occurred. Argentina's right-wing military rulers tortured and murdered lesbian and gay activists: at least 400 of them 'disappeared'. In communist Cuba Fidel Castro denounced homosexuality as a hangover from the corrupt Batista era. Gays were incarcerated in rehabilitation camps from the 1960s and expelled as part of the Mariel exodus of 'social undesirables' in 1983.[17]

More recently, Britain's Conservative Baroness Janet Young continued the Thatcher government's campaign against equality for lesbians and gays. Young's proclaimed aim was to protect the institution of the family. In so doing she was in accord with the former Marxist, fiercely anti-British and anti-gay leader of Zimbabwe, Robert Mugabe.

Scapegoats and authority

The most obvious and simple reason for political leaders of any stripe to wage a campaign against minorities is the oldest in the book: scapegoating. It can be seen in Malaysian leader Mahathir Mohamad's imprisonment of his political opponent Anwar Ibrahim on sodomy charges – and the subsequent rallying of support for Mahathir's ailing government. Zimbabwe's Robert Mugabe, too, beset by economic woes and growing political unrest, has turned upon an array of scapegoats, including gays and white farmers.

The second motif is authoritarianism. Countries that have an authoritarian style of government are almost always more homophobic. The most commonly given psycho-social explanation for this is that social cohesion depends on a certain degree of 'sexual repression' or 'restraint'. In this view, certain forms of sexual behaviour are considered anti-social and must be rejected for the social order to survive. All the political regimes responsible for the examples described in the previous section – be they communist, Maoist, fascist, McCarthyist, militaristic or right-wing conservative – had one thing in common. They bore the stamp of authoritarianism.

Family and gender

Today a similar authoritarian intolerance can be seen in movements that may claim not to be political but have a strong political agenda and impact nonetheless. In the US, right-wing religious organisations that are violently anti-gay are presenting themselves as champions and defenders of the traditional family, taking names like 'Focus on the Family' or the 'Family Research Council'. To them LGBT people are destructive, powerful aggressors. Anthony Falzarano of the Family Research Council says: 'Basically the homosexual... is out to destroy traditional marriage, heterosexual marriage...'.[18]

Although the threat to the family is one of the most common ideological expressions of homophobia, the real objection may have more to do with fixed ideas about gender. Deviation from heterosexual norms is threatening because it seems to challenge the conventional rules governing female and male roles. This might undermine authoritarian control that often relies heavily on clear gender divisions and duties in an ordered society.

The threat of the alternative

Homosexuality in itself may not pose a real threat to any established social order or regime. After all, many regimes of all political shades have tolerated closet homosexuals within their ranks. The real threat, argues historian Jeffrey Weeks, is when sexual minority activities become an alternative way of life:

'When people endorse the idea of sexual pluralism, they are also implicitly endorsing social and political pluralism. When they affirm their lesbian and gay identities, when they assert their sense of belonging to social movements and communities organized around their sexual preferences they are making a political statement. Homosexuality then becomes more than an individual quirk or private choice. It becomes a challenge to absolute values of

all kinds. Authoritarian regimes don't like that.'[19]

The LGBT movement in some states of the US has been very successful in creating social and political space for sexual minority people. San Francisco, New York and many other major cities have bustling sexual minority communities. Lesbians, gays and transsexuals are visible like never before. For some this is cause for alarm. Judith Reisman of the anti-gay Ex-Gay movement warns:

'I would suggest to you, that while the homosexual population may right now be one- or two-per-cent, hold your breath people, because the recruitment is loud: it is clear; it is everywhere. You'll be seeing, I would say, twenty-per-cent or more probably thirty-per-cent, or even more than that of the young population will be moving into homosexual activity.'[20]

The message of these organisations is that homosexuals are dangerous: they want to destroy everything that is dear to you; most of all they want to pervert your children and grandchildren.

It's easy to dismiss views like these as hysterical conspiracy theories. But such organisations provide a logic for hate crimes against LGBT people. And the closing of ranks between various homophobic elements – combined with the political clout they can wield at crucial United Nations conferences to oppose equality for LGBT people – is cause for concern. While there has been some progress in human rights legislation, this should not detract from the fact that persecution blights the lives of hundreds of thousands of sexual minority people around the world today.

Homophobia has been around for a long time. It runs deep and it will take much legislation, awareness, education and practice to root it out. It also requires continued action, commitment and vigilance to stop homophobia destroying lives like that of Matthew Shepard and countless, uncounted, others.

See also **Faith** and **Clitoridectomy**

I

Intersex

'If I am like this, God will know why... If I feel good, why should I want to change things? This is how I grew up, why look for something else?'

Bonny, an intersexual or 'guevedoche', in the Dominican Republic, speaking to Rolando Sanchez in the documentary film 'Guevote'[1]

● ● ●

In many parts of the world there are ongoing campaigns against female genital mutilation (FGM), also known as female circumcision. Human rights organisations decry the practice as a violation of the rights of girls and women. FGM has constituted the grounds for successful asylum applications.

However, there is a form of genital mutilation that continues in most countries of the world today – most prolifically in the rich West. Most of us don't even know it's happening. It takes place in conditions of secrecy, veiled in the respectability of western medical practice. It is usually done to small children, who cannot give their consent, and is carried out legally by medical professionals. Sometimes even parents are not properly informed.

We are talking about intersex genital mutilation – or IGM. In medical circles it is commonly called 'corrective surgery' and it has been practised for over 40 years in most industrialised countries.

'Corrective' surgery - or mutilation?

Intersex people – formerly known as 'hermaphrodites' – are usually born with genitals somewhere between male and female. Such births are far more common than most people imagine. According to the Intersex Society of North America, one in every 2,000 infants is born with ambiguous genitalia which may arise from a number of causes. More than 2,000 'corrective surgeries' on such patients are performed in the US each year.[2] Surgery usually starts on babies under 18 months and may continue throughout the patient's life. It is not uncommon for intersex patients to undergo 30 or more operations, many of them to correct the effects of previous operations.

As children, intersexuals undergo repeated unexplained examinations, surgery, pain and infection. In most cases these children are 'lost to follow-up' by the medical profession. This means there was no reliable medical data to assess the effects of surgery or to provide guidance for future practice.

Social panic

Intersex support and campaign groups on both sides of the Atlantic are at last bringing people together. Their conclusions directly challenge most of the presumptions of the medical profession.

Surgeons admit they are responding to a 'psycho-social emergency' rather than a medical one. Only very rarely are the conditions that they 'correct' life-threatening – or even medically necessary. Some parents may not even have noticed a problem.

This is the usual process: infants born with ambiguous genitals undergo many tests to determine what sex they will be assigned. The decision is based on criteria such as the ability to create cosmetically unambiguous and functional genitals with the tissue present. Genital size is all important. The criteria for normality are: a penis of at least one inch – (2.5cm); a clitoris no larger than a quarter of an inch (0.9cm). Once determination is made, infants are named and a birth certificate filed. The parents are instructed to treat the infant as being of the specified sex, without any ambiguity. Surgery is performed before the age of 18 months to make the genitals match, as closely as possible, the assigned sex. Often surgery is performed on very small babies: girls as young as six weeks may be operated on to deepen their vaginas. And this is only the beginning – often a lifelong road of surgery lies ahead.

In the medical literature, ambiguous genitals are referred to as 'deformed' prior to surgery and 'corrected' after. But the reported experience of intersexuals who went through this in childhood

Cheryl Chase was born 'intersex' in 1956, with ambiguous sexual organs that were operated on. After learning her past, Chase founded the Intersex Society of North America, hoping to end the shame and secrecy surrounding intersex and halt the type of surgery that had left her scarred and unable to have an orgasm, 2000.

© AP Photo/Robert Mecea

suggests quite the opposite. Many report a sense of being 'intact' before surgery and mutilated after it. Their consent was rarely obtained – mostly they were far too young anyway – and frequently they were lied to.

A fairly typical example is recounted by a woman who, when her body began to change at the age of 12, was told she needed surgery to remove her ovaries because she had cancer. What actually happened during the operation was that her clitoris and newly descended testes were removed.[3] This example shows the depths of social panic about gender. What else could induce presumably responsible adults to tell a child she had cancer knowing she did not?

Medical professionals who practise IGM argue that they are only trying to help children and their parents. US Associate Professor of Urology and Paediatrics Laurence Baskin says: 'The majority of these patients have done well... They would never be fertile as a male. They would have a small dysfunctional penis. If you leave a big clitoris they [patients] don't look like a girl. Most patients don't want a clitoris that looks like a penis. People want to look normal. I am trying to help kids.' He adds that having an intersex child is also 'very disturbing to parents'.

On this Cheryl Chase, founder of the Intersex Society of North America, agrees: 'It is very disturbing. And when people are really disturbed, it's not the time to make major, irreversible decisions.'[4]

The Intersex Society does not just oppose surgery. It also proposes that parents receive counselling, and are put in contact with other parents of intersex children. It believes that the child should be assigned a sex, given a name that corresponds to the sex, and raised with age-appropriate explanations of their condition. According to Howard Devore, a San Francisco psychologist who was also born intersexual: 'The child will assert their gender identity between the ages of six and ten.' And there is the ethical issue of consent, as Chase points out:

'The infant is the patient, not the parents! Gender is not so fragile that cosmetic surgery needs to be done early. Gender identity would not be undermined by asking a child about it.'

There are legal issues too. In 1999 the Constitutional Court of Colombia issued two decisions which significantly restrict the ability of parents and doctors to resort to the scalpel when their children are born with atypical genitalia. It was the first time a high court anywhere in the world had considered whether Intersex Genital Mutilation is a violation of human rights. Colombia's court went further by recognising that intersex people are a minority group that enjoys the constitutional protection of the state against discrimination and that every individual has a constitutional right to define his or her own sexual identity. Interestingly, the Colombian court based its ruling on the United Nations Convention on the Rights of the Child. The court said:

'Intersexed people question our capacity for tolerance and constitute a challenge to the acceptance of difference. Public authorities, the medical community and the citizenry at large have a duty to open up a space for these people who have up to now been silenced... We all have to listen to them, and not only to learn to live with them, but

also learn from them' [5]

Sydney Levy of the International Gay and Lesbian Human Rights Commission (IGLHRC) responded: 'We hope that human rights activists around the world will follow the Court's mandate. Mutilation is torture any way you look at it.'

Vive la différence

Intersex children are not rejected or 'corrected' everywhere in the world. Responses to ambiguous genitals vary according to culture – and in less rich, less industrialised and less medicalised countries people tend to be more accepting.

In India the *hijras* have a long history. Known as a 'third gender' caste, *'hijra'* translates as hermaphrodite, or eunuch or 'sacred erotic female-man'. Some are born intersexual, others are castrated. Many contemporary *hijras* work as prostitutes. Others make a living as debt collectors. And some have even gone into politics. One famous *hijra* politician is Shabna Nehru, who claims to belong to both genders but was raised as a girl. According to Nehru, *hijra* status is no obstacle to a political life: 'You need brains for politics. Not genitals.' She also says that *hijras* are less susceptible to nepotistic corruption than more conventional people.[6]

On the other side of world, in the Dominican Republic there is cultural acceptance for gender variance. A rare form of pseudo-hermaphroditism was found among a group of rural villagers in the early 1970s. Twenty-three extended families are affected.[7] The family of intersexual Chi Chi is one of them. In filmmaker Roberto Sanchez's documentary, *Guevote*, Chi Chi's mother explains that of her 10 children, three are girls, three are boys and four are 'of this special sort'. She continues:

'I knew that this sort of thing existed before I had my own kids. But I never thought it would happen to me... I told them to accept their destiny, because God knows what he's doing. And I said real men often achieve less that those who were born as girls. And that's how it turned out. My sons who are real men haven't achieved nearly as much as the others.'

The medical explanation for the phenomenon is that, while still in the womb, some male babies are unable to produce the testosterone which helps external male genitals to develop. They are born with labia-like scrotum, a clitoris-like penis and undescended testes. At first these children were assumed to be female and brought up as such. But because they were genetically male, they began to develop male characteristics at puberty, including penis growth and descending testes. For this reason they are known locally as 'guevedoche' or 'balls at 12'.

Fortunately, these children did not come to the attention of the western medical profession with its obsession with 'corrective surgery'. A research team headed by Julliane Imperato-McGinley did study them and proposed that in a laissez-faire environment with no social intervention, the child would naturally develop a male gender identity at puberty, in spite of having been raised a female. In fact, some did and some didn't. Chi Chi and Bonny did, but a third, Lorenza, did not. As Bonny explains, Lorenza, 'had more chances as a woman. Lots of men fell in love with her. She always wore women's clothes and had very long hair. She liked it when men fell in love with her. That's why she wanted to stay a woman and not become a man.'

The social acceptance of people like Chi Chi in the community is reflected in his words: 'Whatever I feel, that's the way I am. I was born as a girl, and that girl died one day and the boy was born. And the boy was born from that girl in me. I'm proud of who I am. A lot of people really envy us.'

Resisting the scalpel

There is much that the rich, scalpel-happy world might learn from the laissez-faire approach of more tolerant cultures. Activists in the US and Europe are supporting each other in breaking the silence. One man contributing to the UK Intersex Association site only found out as an adult (and after more than 20 painful and distressing operations) that he had a cousin and uncle with the same condition living in the US. No-one in his family had thought to mention it.

In 1994 Cheryl Chase and others began gathering stories into a newsletter called *Hermaphrodites with Attitude*. More people are trying to piece together their own stories of what happened to them as children. Ironically, one of the best examples of the folly of 'corrective surgery' on children is the very example that was supposed to prove its success.

In 1963 a team advised by Professor John Money of Johns Hopkins University, US, did corrective surgery on a baby boy who had lost his penis in a circumcision accident. The boy was given plastic surgery to make his genitals female-like and at puberty was treated with female hormones. Between 1973 and 1975 Money reported a completely favourable outcome and this became the key case in the following two decades of treatment. The child was then, as they say, 'lost to follow-up'.

What actually happened was that, in spite of surgery and upbringing as a girl, the child did not feel like a girl at all. At the age of 12 he discarded the prescribed oestrogen pills. He refused surgery to deepen the vagina that had been made when he was aged 17 months. At the age of 14 he managed to convince local doctors to provide a mastectomy, phalloplasty and male hormones. He now lives as a man.

See also: **Trans Liberation** and XXYY

J.

Judges... and the law

'Sodomy is a crime, for which both partners are punished. The punishment is death if the participants are adults, of sound mind and consenting.'

'The punishment for lesbianism for persons who are mature, of sound mind and consenting, is 100 lashes. If the act is repeated three times and punishment is enforced each time, the death sentence will apply on the fourth occasion.'

Articles 102-113 and Articles 127,129, 130 of Iran's 1991 Islamic penal law. [1]

● ● ●

Laws against homosexuality go back a long way. In 342 AD the Christian Roman Emperor Constantine issued an edict mandating 'exquisite punishment' for men who offered themselves in a 'womanly fashion' to other men. In 533 AD Emperor Justinian of Constantinople extended the death penalty to homosexual acts. Nearly 700 years later a 1207 French statute ordered that a man who engaged in homosexual relations 'shall, on a first offence, lose his testicles and shall lose his member [penis] on a second offence' and that a woman would – mysteriously – 'lose her member each time and on the third must be burned'. In 1533 King Henry VIII introduced the first secular laws against homosexuality to the English speaking world with a law that made buggery punishable by death. Emperor Charles V who ruled the Holy Roman Empire and Spain extended the punishment to women who had sex with each other. Macaulay's Law,

● Fifty-two alleged homosexuals on trial for debauchery, Cairo, Egypt.
November 2001. Their crime was to have a party on a nightclub boat – the *Nile
Queen* – with other consenting gay men. Twenty-one of the men were convicted of
'obscene behaviour between men'. Some of the accused claimed that while in police
custody they were suspended by the wrists, beaten with sticks and subjected to
other forms of torture.[2]

© Rex Features/Sipa Press

passed in Britain in 1861, made homosexuality between men an
imprisonable rather than a capital offence and this was applied
throughout the British empire.[3]

The law now

Today homosexuality is illegal in some 80 states in the world.[4] It is
punishable by death in Iran, Afghanistan, Saudi Arabia, Mauritania,
Sudan, Pakistan, United Arab Emirates, Yemen, and the northern
provinces of Nigeria.[5]

In recent years executions of gay and transgender men have taken place in Afghanistan, Saudi Arabia and Iran. Amnesty International reports that five men convicted of homosexuality in Afghanistan were crushed to death in May 1998 by having a wall collapsed on them. Reuters reports the hanging of a man in Iran for having gay sex in 1998.[6] Three men were executed in Saudi Arabia in January 2002; Amnesty International believes that they were convicted primarily because of their sexual orientation.[7]

In Uganda, Guyana, India, Singapore, Maldives, Bhutan, and Nepal homosexuality may be punished with life imprisonment.[8] Sentences can exceed 14 years in Fiji, Gambia, Kiribati, Kenya,

Some legal milestones

1992-94: Australian gay rights activist Nicholas Toonen brings a complaint against Australia before the UN Human Rights Committee. It finds that a law in the state of Tasmania outlawing homosexuality violates both Toonen's right to privacy and to freedom from discrimination. Tasmania decriminalises homosexuality.

1992: The European Court of Human Rights holds that in order to protect the right to private life, states must take minimum steps towards recognising the sex reassignment of post-operative transsexuals. However, this is very limited in that it does not include an obligation to alter identity documents, recognise marriage or give parental rights.

1993: Following a challenge by gay Irish senator David Norris, the European Court finds Ireland's criminalisation of homosexuality to be in breach of the Convention. Decriminalisation follows.

1996: South Africa, now under majority rule, becomes the first country in the world to include an equality clause in its Constitution that guarantees freedom from discrimination on the grounds of sexual orientation.

1997: the European Union adopts the Treaty of Amsterdam, the first regional human-rights treaty specifically to include a prohibition of discrimination on the basis of sexual orientation. Cases brought to the European Court of Human Rights in Strasbourg cover a range of issues including discriminatory age of consent laws and parental rights.

1998: Ecuador includes prohibition of discrimination based on sexual orientation in its new Constitution. In the late 1990s anti-

Malaysia, Papua New Guinea, Puerto Rico, Solomon Islands, Tanzania, Tuvalu and Zambia. A maximum 10-year sentence applies in Bahrain, Brunei, Burma, Jamaica, Marshall Islands, Qatar, Sri Lanka, Tonga, and Trinidad and Tobago. Some 40 other countries punish same-sex sexual activity with financial penalties, corporal punishment and custodial sentences.[9] Even if the laws are not strictly enforced they create a climate of fear and render gay people especially vulnerable to persecution, attack and extortion.

In countries where same-sex relations are not specifically mentioned in law, other laws may be called upon. For example,

discrimination laws start to appear in a number of Brazilian states.

1999: The European Court and Commission of Human Rights find a breach of the right to privacy in a case where a Portuguese man lost custody of his child on the basis of his homosexuality and was granted access only if he hid his orientation.[10]

2000: The European Charter of Fundamental Rights prohibits discrimination on the grounds of sexual orientation – the first international human rights charter to make such specific reference. It applies to all EU countries.

2002: Article 200 of the Romanian Penal Code, which criminalises same-sex relations, is repealed. It was under this law that Amnesty International's first LGBT prisoner of conscience, Mariana Cetiner, was arrested in October 1995 for 'attempting to seduce another woman', convicted and sentenced to three years imprisonment.[11]

2003: Transgender people in Britain and Japan win the right to marry and have documents reissued according to their new gender identity. In Australia Roz Houston breaks new legal ground when she is awarded damages by the Tasmanian Anti-discrimination Tribunal against neighbours who harassed and physically abused her because she was transgendered.[12]

2003: The US Supreme Court, in the case of Lawrence and Garner v Texas, overturns anti-sodomy laws in Texas as unconstitutional. This landmark ruling invalidates such laws in 12 other US states.[13]

Increasingly anti-discrimination and anti-vilification policies are being adopted by local, municipal or regional authorities in various parts of the world.

Congo uses 'crimes against the family' legislation. Anti-propaganda laws are sometimes exploited (for example in Kuwait and Lebanon) to restrict LGBT people's freedom of speech or right to associate.

Empire and Shari'a

The states with strongest punishments for homosexuality are Muslim countries that apply Shari'a law and former colonies of the British empire, which still base their laws on colonial British legislation.

There are some Muslim-majority countries where homosexuality is not illegal, including Iraq, Jordan, Egypt and Turkey. But that does not necessarily mean that sexual minority people are safe from legal persecution.

The anti-gay tradition in former British colonies is remarkably persistent: some 30 former British colonies or protectorates still criminalise homosexuality. By contrast, homosexuality was rarely illegal under French colonial rule and most of the former colonies of Spain abandoned any anti-gay laws some time ago. While several countries have decriminalised homosexuality in recent years, others have done the opposite. In Fiji, for example, it became illegal again after the 2000 coup. The same happened in Nicaragua when in 1992 President Violeta Chamorro reversed the policies of the previous Sandinista government and outlawed homosexuality.

Transgender people may also find themselves on the wrong side of the law. Gender reassignment (also known as 'sex change') is illegal in Iran, Ghana and Albania.[14] Many countries refuse to reissue official identity documents to reflect sex reassignment of post-operative transsexuals.

Legal activism

But there is another side to the legal coin. Activists all over the world have stepped up their campaigns for legal reform and increasingly seek legal means to fight for their rights. In countries as diverse as Colombia, Hawaii and South Africa activists have won landmark legal victories that have, in turn, helped to bring about changes in cultural attitudes. Others, unable to obtain justice at home, have turned to the international human rights system – its courts, treaties and agreements – to claim their rights.[15]

Police abuses

There have been many failures too, combined with a continuing reluctance to deal with LGBT issues. Discrimination and other abuses against sexual minorities often go unchallenged because of the tendency of governments on all continents to justify them in the name of culture, religion or national sovereignty. Many of the reports received by Amnesty International of torture or ill-treatment of LGBT people in detention come from countries where same-sex relations are outlawed. But even in countries where homosexuality and transgender are legal, rates of violence against LGBT people may be high. This is often perpetrated by officers of the law, especially in Latin America. Amnesty International has dealt with cases of abuse by police in Argentina, Brazil, Colombia, Venezuela and El Salvador. Abuses include killings, rape, beatings and humiliation.

Legal reform isn't everything. Social attitudes also need to change. But the law is a start and a recourse for those at risk. Laws that treat LGBT individuals as equal citizens with equal rights send out a clear message both to sexual minority people and to those who would abuse them.

See also: **Equality and Homophobia**

K

Kertbeny
and the 'birth of the homosexual'

'I became one of the stately homos of England'
Quintin Crisp, wit, raconteur and author of The Naked Civil Servant[1]

Although same-sex sex has always happened, 'homosexuality' is a comparatively modern idea.

The word was invented in the 1860s by German-Hungarian Karoly Maria Kertbeny (born Benkert in 1824) in a letter to fellow gay rights pioneer Karl Heinrich Ulrichs, and followed up in two pamphlets calling for reform of laws relating to same-sex sex. Kertbeny's word ('homosexualität') is a compound of the Greek word *homo* (same) and the medieval Latin *sexualis* (sexual). The word 'homosexual' did not appear in the English language until 1891, when John Addington Symonds used the phrase 'homosexual instincts' in his book *A Problem in Modern Ethics*. Some people have identified 1869 as the birth date of 'the homosexual' as a type of person and 'homosexuality' as an identity. Up until then there were just same-sex acts which were seen as customs or sins or crimes.

We don't know a great deal about Kertbeny's life except that he was a writer, translator, journalist and polemicist. He appears to have died of syphilis in 1882. He claimed to be a 'Normalsexualer' or heterosexual, but his anonymous and pseudonymous campaign for gay rights suggests he may have been secretly gay.[2]

Kertbeny was not, however, the first to conceive of an individual with desires for their own sex as a specific type of person. In 1864 Ulrichs had published his researches on *The Riddle of Man-Manly*

Two women in bed, by J.A.Rohne (19th century).

Love. Inspired by the science of contemporary embryology, and using the language of Greek mythology, he came up with names for different types of person: a homosexual male was an Urning; a lesbian was an Urningin. A heterosexual male was a Dioning and a heterosexual female was a Dioningin. Ulrichs argued that same-sex desire was congenital and that it was inhumane for the law to punish homosexuals as though these were wilfully chosen crimes.

Ulrichs was imprisoned, ridiculed in the press, forced to leave his native Hanover, and his collection of homosexual research material was confiscated. But his pioneering work had got others thinking.

Ulrichs' aim was to legitimate homosexuality. But that was not the intention of all researchers. Many seemed more interested in pathologising homosexuality and contributing to the continued repression of those who did not fit the heterosexual mould. Ulrichs complained:

'My scientific opponents are mostly doctors of the insane... for example, Westphal, Krafft-Ebing, Stark. They have observed Urnings in lunatic asylums. They have apparently never seen

mentally healthy Urnings. The published views of doctors for the insane are accepted by the others'.[3]

Homosexuality came increasingly to be viewed as a medical condition. In the later 19th century the term 'invert' became popular, following the publication in 1897 of *Sexual Inversion* by British sexologist Havelock Ellis together with John Addington Symonds (though the latter's name was removed from the title page after the first edition). This popularised the notion that 'inversion' was an inborn pathological gender anomaly.

In the early years of the 20th century British socialist and gay pioneer Edward Carpenter published his polemical book *The Intermediate Sex* which was to have a profound effect upon women as well as men. Feminist Frances Wilder wrote to him in 1915:

'I have recently read with interest your book entitled The Intermediate Sex *and it has lately dawned on me that I myself belong to that class and I write to ask of there is a any way of getting in touch with others of the same temperament.'*

But it was the term 'homosexual' that was to be the most durable scientific term, used internationally from Brazil to India. It is not, however, always popular with gay people. In the 1950s 'homophile' and 1970s 'gay and lesbian' communities the term homosexual was rejected because of the medical and clinical connotations it had acquired. Today many still prefer other terms with which to describe themselves – 'gay' or 'lesbian' or the reclaimed label 'queer', for example.

See also: **Against nature, Gay gene, Clitoridectomy and** Queer

L

Love...
that dare not speak its name

'should I tell you

my hidden truth

of years and centuries

Holding you, then,

Should I cross the black fear?

Should I say it in words?'
From *For You* by Maya Sharma[1]

The place, London's Old Bailey. The date, 26 April to 1 May. The year 1895. This is the first criminal trial of Oscar Wilde. He and a certain Arthur Taylor, described as procurer of young men for the playwright and wit, are facing 25 counts of gross indecency and conspiracy to commit gross indecency. It is the most high-profile trial of its kind in memory. It is also one of the wittiest and saddest. And its most famous line is not even Wilde's, but comes from a poem written by his lover, Lord Alfred Douglas, aka 'Bosie'. At one point in the trial, leading prosecutor Charles Gill reads out the poem 'Two Loves'. The two loves are personified – the one type is heterosexual. It claims:
'I am the True Love, I fill
The hearts of girl and boy with mutual flame'

The other type of love sighs and replies:

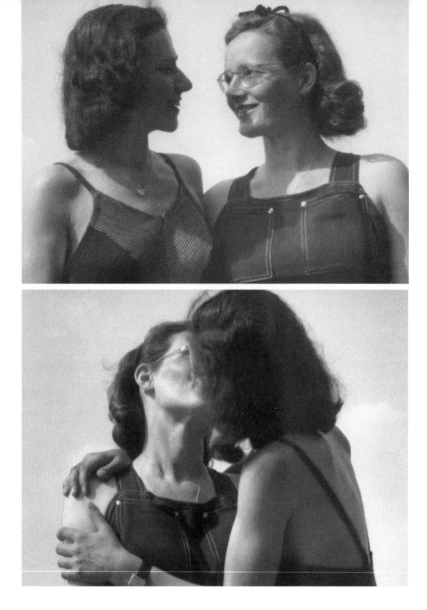

Felice Schragenheim and Elisabeth 'Lilly' Wust, Berlin, August 1944. At the beginning of their relationship, Elisabeth, mother of four and wife of a Nazi officer stationed at the front, did not know that Felice was a Jew living underground. When she found out, Elisabeth was forced to confront her own ingrained anti-Semitism. The two women lived together, but eventually Felice was revealed to the Gestapo and deported to the ghetto of Theresienstadt. Elisabeth tried in vain to join her there. It was only several years after the war's end that she learned that Felice had been sent to Bergen-Belsen, where she died in 1945. Their story was told in the documentary film *Aimée and Jaguar*.

' ... Have they will,
I am the love that dare not speak its name'

Gill asks Wilde whether he knows what is meant by this. Wilde replies that he thinks the meaning is clear.

Gill: Is it not clear the loves described relate to natural love and unnatural love?

Wilde, who has hitherto denied the claims against him as lies and blackmail, replies 'No'.

Gill: What is the 'love that dare not speak its name'?

Wilde: The 'love that dare not speak its name' in this century is such a great affection of an elder for a younger man as there was between David and Jonathan, such as Plato made the very basis of his philosophy... It is that deep spiritual affection that is as pure as it is perfect. It dictates and pervades great works of art like those of Shakespeare and Michelangelo... It is in this century misunderstood, so much misunderstood that it may be described as 'the love that dare not speak its name', and on account of it I am placed where I am now. It is beautiful, it is fine, it is the noblest form of affection. There is nothing unnatural about it... The world mocks at it and sometimes puts one on the pillory for it...'.[2]

At this point the courtroom erupts into loud applause mingled with some hisses. The judge calls for silence and says he will have the court cleared 'if there is the slightest manifestation of feeling'.

Eloquent and memorable though it was, Wilde's defence did not stand up to the evidence of male prostitutes, hotel staff and others, and he was sentenced to two years' hard labour. He was later to renounce his homosexuality, saying it was a 'madness' that had afflicted him. On his release from Reading Gaol he fled to France, dying there aged 46, a broken man.

The three Wilde trials were dramatic and significant because they created a public image for homosexuals and were held up as a terrifying morality tale of the dangers of deviant behaviour.[3] The phrase 'the love that dare not speak its name' was especially resonant because it played upon the way in which silence had been used throughout the centuries to squash and oppress homosexual love.

The Apostle Paul set the tone when he addressed the Ephesians (5:12): 'for it is a shame to speak of the things that they do in secret.' Shame, it seems, attached to the teller as well as the perpetrator. In 1700, the Italian Ludovico Sinutrari d'Ameno told of 'silent sin and un-nameable vice' – designating sodomy.[4] In 1769 the influential English jurist Sir William Blackstone described the 'crime against nature' as 'a subject the very mention of which is a disgrace to human nature' and 'a crime not fit to be named'.[5] Even in much 20th century literature or film homosexuality could not be named. Often it was alluded to with unfinished sentences: 'Is she, you know... that way?' Or euphemisms, used originally by homosexual people themselves, as in: 'Is he a friend of Dorothy's?'

When the Sexual Offences Act of 1967 finally decriminalised homosexuality in Britain, its sponsors made it clear that this was tolerance – not acceptance:

'Any form of ostentatious behaviour now, or in the future, any form of public flaunting would be truly distasteful and would, I believe, make the sponsors of the Bill regret that they have done what they have done. Homosexuals must remember that while there is nothing bad in being a homosexual, there is certainly nothing good.' [6]

Given this background, it is perhaps unsurprising that when gay lib did break out it was anything but silent. Indeed, the breaking of silence became an integral, political part of gay pride. Or as one wit had it: 'The love that dared not speak its name... now can scarcely ever shut up!'

Hitting the mainstream

Since the 1980s, mainstream western culture has accepted gay and transgender themes in films, books and music like never before. *The Crying Game, Aimée and Jaguar, Torchsong Trilogy, Show Me Love* are just a few examples of films that have reached a mass market. It has also become much easier for people in the public eye to be open about their sexuality. Whereas it would have been professional suicide for a movie star like Rock Hudson to reveal his true nature in the 1940s or 1950s, the careers of actors like Ian McKellen and Jodie Foster have continued apparently unharmed by their sexuality becoming public knowledge.

However, many actors are still reluctant to let their love 'speak its name' for fear that they will become typecast, lose their 'mass appeal', and spoil their chances of getting the far more plentiful straight parts. In spite of the comparatively positive coverage that sitcom star Ellen DeGeneres received for her very public 'coming out' on her TV show, her ratings subsequently declined and she was soon dropped off the listings. There remain a great many people in Hollywood, and show business in general, who for strictly professional reasons would rather their love kept quiet.

Musicians seem to fare rather better. Melissa Etheridge, Boy George, Elton John, George Michael (some reluctantly 'outed') have all made their contributions to increasing social acceptability of homosexuality, bisexuality and transgender. More than this, homosexuality has in some places become positively fashionable – as demonstrated by the Russian duo and 2003 Eurovision Song Contest entrants, t.A.T.u. Doubts have even been expressed as to whether the pair, Yulia Volokova and Lena Katina, really are lesbians or are just pretending to be! It's a far cry from the 1960s when superstar Dusty Springfield had to keep her lesbianism tightly under wraps. Meanwhile, even the homophobic rap of presumably heterosexual stars like Eminem, Icecube and others, has provoked a queer counter-culture, with gay, lesbian and bisexual hip-hop artists like Mz Platinum, God-Des, Johnny Dangerous, Fat Rat and Caushun giving out a different message. Dutchboy, who heads the band Rainbow Flava, sings:

'Struggling every goddamn day/Cuz I decide to be real/Got to be who I am – a gypsy queen!'

Today, as the annual round of LGBT Pride marches take place in cities around the world, transforming the streets into a great carnival of noise and colour, it's easy to forget the many victims of silence who still suffer. Indian poet Sandhya reminds us:

'Fifteen years ago my lover died, she was very young, and so was I. At that time I did not know another breathing lesbian in this country. I could not tell my parents, my family or my straight friends about my grief. Silence was the only possible refuge. I betrayed our time together in many ways by not talking about us, and our love. Fifteen years later, I look at these poems written in a secret diary – the only safe space for that pain. I feel rage that I let the world shut me up. And that I continue to let it shut me up.'[7]

See also: Judges and Equality

M
●　●

Marriage

'What are you trying to protect marriage from? There isn't a
limited amount of love in Iowa. It isn't a non-renewable resource. If
Amy and Barbara or Mike and Steve love each other, it doesn't
mean that John and Mary can't.'

State Representative Ed Fallon, opposing legislation that prohibits recognition of gay
marriages performed in other states.[1]

In December 1996 the Malaysian press was abuzz with the
sensational story of a 21-year-old woman in the state of Kelantan. She
had impersonated a man in order to marry her lover, another woman.
Hailed as the first incident of its kind in Malaysian history, the case
continued to be newsworthy for well over three months. Every angle
of the story was explored.

The accused, Azizah Abdul Rahman, was said to have fooled
everyone: her bride, Rohana, the local imam or religious leader, the
district registrar of marriages, and the witnesses at her wedding.

All professed that they had no idea that Azizah was a woman. Not
only did she look and behave like a man, she also had assumed a
man's name and possessed a male ID card. Within three weeks of her
arrest she was indicted and sentenced to two years' imprisonment on
two counts: the first, and more severe charge, was impersonating a
man and the second was using another person's ID card.

Media coverage of the case of Azizah and Rohana ran and ran,
with detailed descriptions of what she looked like (more like a boy

Cesar Gigliutti and Marcelo Suntheim are greeted by wellwishers outside Buenos Aires' City Hall, Argentina, 18 July 2003. Their marriage ceremony is the first civil union of a gay couple in Latin America.

than a man) and what she'd been wearing (brown slacks and a purple shirt). The marriage registrar was quoted as saying that the incident was perhaps a sign that the world was coming to an end.

As a result of the case the state government announced it would tighten Islamic Family Enactment legislation to prevent marriages between women occurring.[2]

Old customs

Marriage between members of the same sex may be more newsworthy these days, but it's certainly not new. It existed in Ancient Rome, though it was thought to have disappeared until the 20th century. The work of anthropologists, however, has revealed several examples of 'customary marriage' coming from a range of different cultures.

In former Dahomey, now Benin, anthropologist Herskovits found evidence of women marriages between Amazon warriors of the king of Fon. More recently, anthropologist Saskia Wieringa made contact with a local woman who was trying to research this – in spite of the disapproval of her family and threats from her husband. This woman revealed that her grandmother had in fact had two wives. History tells that the Amazons of Fon were disbanded after the French conquest of Abomey in 1894, referred to by Audre Lorde in her poem *125th Street and Abomey.*

In Lesotho, also, voluntary marriages between women were not uncommon into the 1950s, often alongside compulsory heterosexual marriages to men. Anthropologist Judith Gay wrote in 1985: 'elderly informants told me that special affective and gift exchange partnerships among girls and women existed "in the old days" of their youth.' From Mpho Nthunya's account in her 1997 book *Singing Away the Hunger: The autobiography of an African Woman* it would appear that long-term, loving, intimate and erotic relationships between women were the norm in rural Lesotho at that time and were publicly acknowledged and honoured with feasting and celebration. It seems to be a matter of shame to younger generations. Gay describes how when three elderly women were describing this they were interrupted by a 24-year-old daughter-in-law clapping her hands:

"Why are you clapping so?" asked a straightforward 97-year-old woman. "Haven't you ever fallen in love with another girl?"

Today such relationships – or at least their cultural and social acceptance – no longer seem to exist.'[3]

Human right to marry

The Universal Declaration of Human Rights states that all men and women have the right to marry and found a family. Banning marriage involving same-sex couples or transgender people would appear to constitute discrimination in the right to private and family life as well as denying the principle of equality before law.

On the face of it, the human-rights standards do not exclude the idea of same-sex marriage. But up to now human-rights bodies have interpreted the concept of marriage as strictly heterosexual. In the domestic law of most countries marriage is defined as a union between a man and woman. This restriction, it is increasingly argued, denies the human rights of gay people.

Refusing to recognise same-sex relationships in law is more than symbolic. It can have far-reaching and cruel consequences.

Lack of recognition can affect access to a partner undergoing medical treatment. There have been heartrending cases where homophobic families have been able to prevent a gay partner from seeing their dying or critically-ill loved one in hospital. It can make gay people, denied the right to take over housing tenancy, homeless on the death of their partner. Lack of recognition impinges on entitlement to inherit and rights to spousal employment benefits, pensions and tax benefits.

Largely as the result of campaigns by activist groups, same-sex relationships are beginning to gain legal recognition in a growing number of countries and states around the world.

The first legal recognition of same-sex couples occurred in Denmark in 1989, when the state allowed LGBT citizens to register their relationships in a civil ceremony that brought many of the rights associated with marriage. These included rights of property, inheritance, immigration, taxation, and social security. Since then more countries have introduced legal recognition of gay relationships, though it has been a very slow, piecemeal process. Often measures have sparked protest, especially from religious organisations and right-wing extremist groups.

'They have stolen marriage. [That is now] the moral issue of our civilization,' was the response from Traditional Values Coalition head the Reverend Lou Sheldon, following a 1993 Hawaii Supreme Court ruling that preventing gay marriage was discrimination on the grounds of sex.

In 2001 the Netherlands became the first state in the world to open the existing institution of full civil marriage to same-sex partners. Belgium followed suit, then Canada in 2003. More than 20 countries or local authorities have enacted some form of legislation that gives legal recognition to same-sex couples. These include: France, Finland, Germany, Greenland, Hungary, Iceland, Norway, Sweden and some states in the USA. Some municipalities in Britain have a civil-partnerhip register but this has no legal standing.[4]

In South Africa, although gays have won equal rights for same-sex partners under the state health and pension plans, gay rights groups have been careful not to push for state-recognised gay marriage for fear of provoking religious groups and the right-wing lobby. Nor has the ruling party, the ANC, been ready to pass pro-gay equality legislation, in spite of the country's constitutional commitment.

Gay groups in Brazil have taken a bolder approach: in 1995 groups in Rio and the state of Bahia backed their demand for recognition of same-sex relationships with a threat to name 18 gay people in Congress and 50 in the local Catholic Church. Legislation to create civil-union contracts for same-sex couples followed.[5]

Whether recognised by law or not, many LGBT people have gay 'weddings' all the same. In December 2002 Brenda Fassie, South Africa's tempestuous Queen of Pop, 'married' her lover Sindi Nkambule in a spectacular gay wedding in Yeoville, Johannesburg.[6] Others have sought religious ceremonies. Quakers have been conducting blessings for several years, but similar events in the Anglican Church in Canada provoked fierce controversy.

In some countries transgender people have been denied the right to marry in their new gender identity. Some post-operative transsexuals have even been ordered by a court to divorce their now same-sex spouses. But in some cases the ban has been a curious advantage. For example, when a British male-to-female transsexual wanted to marry her lesbian lover in the late 1990s she was able to do so because her birth certificate still identified her as a male. Her lesbian partner wore a smart suit while, she, the male-to-female transsexual, was garbed in full, flowing traditional wedding dress.

Equality – without frills

Views on marriage within LGBT communities are divided. Some see it as a legal and symbolic right that must be fought for and won. Others view marriage as an oppressive institution which mimics heterosexual norms and has mainly negative associations. Gay people have suffered for centuries from rigid notions of the importance of marriage and the nuclear family. Many argue that non-discrimination and equality legislation, regardless of marital status or gender or sexual orientation, is a more appropriate way forward.

See also: **Not in our culture, Judges, Equality and Vegetarian sisterhoods**

Not in our culture

'The enemy is still trying to come back with sinister manoeuvres and tricks called lesbians and homosexuality and globalisation.... They colonised us and now they claim human rights when we condemn and reject them. In Namibia there will be no lesbian and homosexual left. Those who want to [continue with homosexual activities] must pack [up] and go back to Europe.'

President Nujoma of Namibia speaking to SWAPO supporters outside the Okuryangava Women's Centre, Windhoek, on 23 April, 2001[1]

Poliyana Mangwiro was 14 years old when she realised she was 'a woman who loved women'. But she didn't tell anyone:

'I was not sure what was going on with me. I didn't know this word "lesbians". Nobody in the rural area where I lived would have known it.'

So Poliyana did what most rural girls do in Zimbabwe: she got married. By the time she was 17 she had two children. At the age of 20 she ran away from her husband and went to the capital, Harare. There she joined the newly formed lesbian and gay organisation called GALZ (Gays and Lesbians of Zimbabwe). She was volunteering for the organisation at the 1995 Harare International Book Fair when the stall was attacked by an anti-gay group. The incident was widely publicised. Poliyana's picture was splashed over

Deepa Mehta, left, director of the film *Fire*, participates in a candlelight vigil outside the Regal Theatre in New Delhi, India, 7 December 1998. *Fire* has been pulled from theatres and cinemas across India after protests against the film's subject matter (a relationship between two lesbian women) disrupted showings.

the papers and she began to receive threats. For safety, she left Harare and went back to her village. But her notoriety had preceded her and she was rejected by her community. 'They said I did not belong there because I was gay and that was for white people.' Poliyana insists, however, that 'lesbian or gay is part of our culture. There is even a word in our Shona language for it: *ngochani*'.[2] An outspoken defender of gay and lesbian rights in Zimbabwe, Poliyana Mangwiro died of AIDS in 2001.

Claims that homosexuality is 'not part of our culture' are common. Often it has been described as somebody else's disease or sin or crime or custom or problem. As a foreign thing that threatens to pollute the purity of the nation, community, race or class. Old Testament Jews dubbed lesbianism the 'Egyptian vice'; 16th century Spanish missionaries called sodomy 'the Japanese vice' or the 'sin of the Caribs'. For centuries Arabs blamed homosexuality on the Persians.

Such thinking is still very much alive today, especially in parts of Africa and Asia. It forms a potent mix – homophobia and xenophobia. By their very existence gay and lesbian Africans and

Asians and their organisations are challenging this. Reactions against them can be ferocious: LGBT groups are seen as an example of Western corruption; the homosexual citizen is cast as an outsider, a threat to the culture, an enemy (or an agent of the enemy) who must be expelled. And expulsions have happened, either forcibly as in Uganda, or coercively by pushing gay citizens to seek exile and asylum, as in Zimbabwe and Namibia.

Many African leaders have come out with politically charged anti-gay statements and policies. They include Sam Nujoma of Namibia, Robert Mugabe in Zimbabwe, Yoweri Museveni in Uganda and Frederick Chiluba in Zambia. Former Kenyan President Daniel Arap Moi put the commonly held view most succinctly: 'Homosexuality is against African norms and traditions.'[3]

The popular press in these countries has been quick to pick up the message with opinion pieces describing homosexuality as a 'white thing' imposed on blacks, contributing to the damage and decay of black culture. Zimbabwe's Mrs Mangwe, leader of ZANU's Women's League, explained it thus: 'Our way is to protect our culture. Not destroy it by allowing homosexuality to run rife in it. It's not in our black culture and we don't want it.'[4]

African gay traditions

Researchers, however, have shown that homosexuality long preceded colonialism in Africa. According to anthropologist Edward Evans-Pritchard, this and other forms of same-sex eroticism were indigenous. Two thousand-year-old cave paintings of the Southern African San people show men copulating. In warrior cultures especially there are indications of sexual relationships between men. And there are traditions of women marrying each other in several African countries including Ghana, Lesotho and Kenya.

Among Azande people, living in what is today south-western Sudan, northern DR Congo, and the south-eastern corner of the Central African Republic, a form of intergenerational homo-eroticism was practised long ago and until the beginning of the 20th century. Azande women also practised same-sex eroticism. Transgendered homosexuality is documented among Nuba people in Sudan. There were names for men engaging in homosexual eroticism and even same-sex marriages, according to anthropologist SF Nadel. Homosexual and transgendered males had roles as spiritual functionaries among a number of African cultures – including the

Longo people of Uganda, Murus of Kenya, Ilas of Zambia and Zulu people of South Africa.[5]

The claim that homosexuality is un-African is 'a lie', says South African activist and writer Shuaib Rahim. 'The actual European imperialist import is the homophobic tradition of British law.' He recalls how when he and fellow gays were growing up in apartheid South Africa they were called many bad names:

'But perhaps worst of all we were called "un-African". The first of my ancestors came to Africa in the 17th century. They came from all over – including Java, Malaysia, Denmark and India. Our family has lived in this country since then. And I am a "moffie" [derogatory Afrikaans word for gay]. Does that make me un-African? I must admit that I thought that it did... [then] I started reading about our history and discovered many interesting facts. Simon Nkoli was a great hero of the liberation struggle. An ANC activist, he spent four years in prison under apartheid. While in prison he "came out" as a moffie to his fellow inmates and was accepted. After his release he became the face of struggle for lesbian and gay rights in Africa. I dare anyone to tell me that Simon Nkoli was not African in every sense of the word.'[6]

Hindu gay heritage

With gay and lesbian activism increasing in Africa and Asia, LGBT issues are increasingly in the spotlight. The furore caused in India by the lesbian film *Fire* received international coverage. Deepa Mehta's tale of two women, married to two brothers, developing a relationship with each other in the congested streets of middle-class New Delhi, was passed by the Censor Board. But Hindu extremists attacked a cinema showing it and conservative parliamentarians had a field day condemning it. Pramod Navalkar, Minister of Culture in the state of Maharashtra, told newspapers that lesbianism was 'a pseudo-feminist trend from the West and no part of Indian womanhood'.

Such provocations, however, produced a tremendous and unprecedented 'coming-out' of Indian lesbians who took to the streets in protest. Ashwini Sukthanker relates: 'Hundreds of people showed up. For the first time ever, lesbians were visible... In the sea of placards about human rights, secularism, women's autonomy, freedom of speech, was the sign painted in the colours of the national flag: "Indian and lesbian". Who would have thought that staking such a saucy claim to our national pride would result in such a furore?'

But it did. The deputy editor of the weekly *India Today* expressed particular dismay that 'the militant gay movement, which has hitherto operated as website extensions of a disagreeable trend in the West, could not come out into the open and flaunt banners in Delhi suggesting that "lesbianism is part of our heritage".' He went on: 'Thievery, deceit, murder and other...[criminal offences] have a long history. That does not elevate them to heritage.'[7]

The attempt to negate or even obliterate any positive tradition of homosexuality in India has precendents. From the 1920s to the 1940s Mahatma Gandhi led a campaign to erase all positive references to transgenderism and same-sex desire in Indian, especially Hindu, culture. During those years, Gandhi sent out squads of his devotees to destroy the erotic representations, especially homo-erotic and lesbian ones, carved on Hindu temples dating from the 11th century.[8]

Writer and philosopher Rabindranath Tagore was able to halt this violent action. Nevertheless the campaign to erase the history of gender and sexual variance was continued by Prime Minister Jawaharlal Nehru, who held office from 1946 to 1964. Like Gandhi he had been educated in England, and like him he wished to convey the message that it was the English who had brought homosexuality to India. He was upset when his friend Alain Daniélou published photographs of traditional Hindu sculptures depicting homo-eroticism and transgender people. The thousands-strong community of transgendered *hijras* (or eunuchs) have a tradition within Indian culture stretching back 2,000 years.

Gay in the Muslim world

'Culture is not always against us and there are positive examples of same-sex relationships to be found in different Muslim cultures,' writes Anissa Helie.[9] She cites the example of traditional travelling theatres and musical groups in Pakistan, where male couples live out their relationships quite openly and points to a body of local and Urdu literature that is clearly based on male love, *yaari*.

British Muslim Raza Griffiths writes of the contemporary scene: 'Despite the impression created by executions of homosexuals in hardline Islamic states... in most Muslim countries, Muslims, especially men, have considerable freedom to have gay sex in private so long as they don't openly come out as gay.'[10]

Several LGBT organisations have been formed in recent years, some under difficult conditions. The group Homan advocates the rights of Iranian gays and lesbians and has branches in the US, Britain, Norway and Sweden. It publishes a web magazine in Farsi and English at www.homan.cwc.net. Al-Fatiha – meaning the 'Opening' or 'Beginning' in Arabic – holds international conferences and has branches in the US, Canada and Britain. In the words of one spokesperson: 'We as gay Muslims who are marginalised can re-awaken the spirit of love within Islam'.

In spite of the protestations of their leaders and their media, 'not part of our culture' simply doesn't ring true for thousands of LGBT people around the world.

See also: **Against nature, Faith, Judges, Homophobia and** Vegetarian **sisterhoods**

O

Out

'Next came the task of telling the parents. I was terrified! I remember one night, I was sitting at the table watching tele. My dad was in the kitchen, and I heard him say "All gays are sick. They should die." I was quite confused, because that statement came out of nowhere. I asked him why he thought this, and he couldn't really answer. I was crushed. That delayed my coming-out for months. Finally, one day I'd had enough. I broke down. I kept telling them "I need to tell you something!" but I couldn't say it. They finally figured it out, I guess, and my mom said: "Are you gay?" and I said: "Yes". They didn't freak, and took it well. I think my mom is uncomfortable discussing it with me, and that upsets me.'

C, a transgender bisexual 17-year-old living in a small town in North Carolina, US.[1]

It's a curious expression: 'coming out'. It used be what well-to-do young ladies of a certain class did as they were formally launched onto the marriage market. But by the mid-20th century it had a rather different connotation. It meant declaring one's homosexuality – and the place to 'come out' of was 'the closet' (or cupboard) where things are normally kept from sight.

There were good reasons for hiding homosexuality. In most countries it was, for men at any rate, illegal and imprisonable. For

A woman holds up a placard during a protest about sexual orientation at the World Conference Against Racism in Durban, September 2001

© AFP Photo/Anna Zieminski

both men and women it was a source of shame that needed to be kept a secret, not only to protect gay individuals, but also their family and acquaintances. This remains the case in many societies and communities around the world today.

In the West, however, during the 1960s and 1970s many countries decriminalised homosexuality. A culture of greater sexual permissiveness prevailed. And the emergence of the gay liberation movement entailed a mass 'coming out' for many people. The mood of the times is captured by British writer Elizabeth Wilson:

'With revivalist fervour, the Gay Liberation Front clamoured onto the streets, wore extravagant clothes, spray-painted psychiatric institutions (including the one where I worked) with slogans, invaded bookstores selling anti-gay books and demonstrated gay pride in an endless round of public events'.[2]

Personal and political

Coming out is also an intensely personal matter. It's that moment when an individual feels they can or have to tell someone about themselves; that moment of truth and release of tension. US teenager C says:

'I feel better about myself, and I don't feel like I'm lying anymore. I was going to snap if I waited any longer... I think I would have committed suicide if I hadn't... so... I'm still alive, and a tremendous weight has been lifted from me.'[3]

But it's not always a positive experience. British 14-year-old Jack says:

'I wanted to be open and proud, but with it came much homophobia... Being stalked by people, being told how sick and disgusting I am, being told that I'm wrong and should have never been born... I feel more miserable about it than I ever have before.'[4]

In families or communities where homosexuality or transgender are viewed as sinful and deeply shameful, coming out may strain relations to the limit. But it also directly challenges the prejudice that causes so much pain and suffering to sexual minority people. For this reason 'coming out' remains one of the most effective ways of bringing about change in social attitudes. In the words of tennis champion Martina Navratilova:

'The more people come out, the less it will be an issue. If we are ashamed of ourselves, how the hell can we expect the rest of the world not to be ashamed of us?'[5]

Popular celebrities who come out as gay or transgender can provide much encouragement for all sexual minority people, especially if the experience has been positive for them. Rocker Melissa Etheridge told *The Advocate*:

'What happened to me is exactly the opposite of what closeted

*people fear; they think they'll lose everything if they come out. This
didn't happen to me at all. In fact everything came back tenfold.'*[6]

Locks on the closet

For most ordinary lesbian or gay people, who do not enjoy celebrity
status, coming out is something that cannot be done just the once. It
may have to be repeated time and again – virtually every time they
meet someone new. There remain huge obstacles for many people in
coming out: personal, environmental, cultural or economic. In poorer
countries of the world, where wages are low and there is rarely an
effective state welfare system, the independent lifestyle enjoyed by
many lesbian and gay people in the West is out of the question.

The family is not only the basic unit of societies, it is also the
economic safety net. But the traditional family is not generally
speaking a safe place for sexual minorities, especially where there are
strong social, cultural or religious rules concerning sex or gender. The
shame brought upon a family by 'sexual deviancy' can inspire
appalling acts of violence. Lesbian or transgender females may be
raped, beaten, forced into marriage. Males may be viciously attacked
to have their homosexuality 'beaten out' of them by family members.

'Coming out' in a hostile environment can cost a person their
family, their job, even their life. Not surprisingly many sexual
minority people in poor countries end up homeless and reliant on
prostitution for survival. Most survive in urban settings where family
bonds are weaker. Cities are, for many sexual minority people, a
salvation. And those who are 'out' in these urban settings have the
potential to change attitudes of the people they come into contact
with.

Out South

The organisation of LGBT people into social, support and campaign
groups in the cities of the global South is highly significant. Hundreds
of these groups have emerged in recent years, even in countries where
homosexuality is illegal. Many have been hounded by the authorities:
Entre Amigos in Salvador, GALZ in Zimbabwe and The Rainbow
Coalition in Namibia, to name but a few.

But these organisations offer a lifeline to thousands. Telephone
helplines regularly counsel people who are suicidal, who feel they are
alone in the world and can see no escape from their predicament.
Internet sites accessible in countries where there are no local groups

'When you come out it does not only concern you and your mother and father. It is a concern of the whole extended family! It means the involvement of thirty of forty people! That is why it is so difficult for us blacks to come out. It is not an individual concern.'
A gay Zimbabwean.[7]

'I'm coming out
I want the world to know
Got to let it show'
Diana Ross

can also put isolated individuals in touch with a wider community of people like them.

'Coming out' can help break silence and encourage people who feel deeply isolated. The existence of a gay scene, wherever in the world it may be, provides opportunities for LGBT people to meet, start relationships and enjoy a sense of belonging, be it over the snooker table, in the opera house, at a demo or on a gay hike. When you are out on the scene with other LGBT people you can just be; you don't have to 'come out', time and time again.

See also: Stonewall and Youth

P
● ●

Positive lives

'The greatest challenge lies ahead: the challenge of saving millions of lives by expanding access to AIDS treatment to all those who need it, while simultaneously fighting the social and economic forces that have accelerated the spread of HIV/AIDS.'
Zackie Achmat, South African Aids activist[1]

● ● ●

In the eyes of many, Zackie Achmat comes close to being a saint. The gay ex-prostitute and HIV-activist hit the headlines in 2001 by refusing to take anti-retrovirals (drugs that tackle the symptoms of AIDS and can prolong life) until they were available for everyone in his country, South Africa.

In doing so he presented a poignant, personal challenge to President Thabo Mbeki's controversial AIDS policy. Mbeki, unconvinced of the link between HIV and AIDS, was refusing to make anti-retrovirals widely available through the national health system. As a result, many have died and pregnant women have helplessly passed on HIV to their babies, while knowing that drugs exist to prevent this happening.

On a hospital visit to Achmat, Nelson Mandela controversially declared him 'a role model' and said 'his action is based upon a fundamental principle which we all admire'.[2] At the time Achmat was bedridden with acute bronchitis, one of the infections that regularly threaten his life as his immune system collapses.

Achmat, and the Treatment Action Campaign he heads, won an

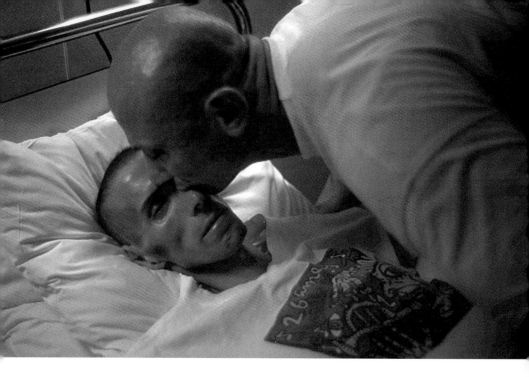

● Positive lives ... artist photographer Gotscho kisses his lover, Gilles Dusein, as he dies of AIDS (Paris 1993). Dusein was a prominent photographic dealer who promoted the work of many photographers.

© Nan Goldin

agreement with the South African government that includes plans to reduce mother-to-child transmission by a fifth by 2005 and reduce infection rates among 15- to 24-year-olds through the dispensing of drugs. Nonetheless, in February 2003 South African activists launched a campaign of civil disobedience, saying that the government's continued reluctance to make anti-retrovirals widely available was costing an estimated 600 lives a day.[3]

'Gay plague'

When AIDS first made its impact in the 1980s it quickly became known as the 'gay plague'. This was because it seemed to hit the gay community in San Francisco the hardest. What followed was a reaction against gays, lesbians and bisexuals who were accused of bringing the threat of AIDS to the population at large.

The response from the gay and lesbian community was swift, direct and un-prudish. Safer-sex messages were made loudly and clearly. AIDs was not to be 'hushed up'. 'Silence = death' became the popular activist slogan. The struggle to get healthcare for a

> **My daughter was raped when she was six because of my coming out and telling people about HIV. They were trying to shut my mouth. But they didn't stop me. I was only happy that she was not infected...**
> Joyce, an HIV-positive South African lesbian.[4]

marginalised (and now especially stigmatised) group led to an upsurge in community-based activism among lesbian and gay people. The fact that politically aware gay and lesbian communities already existed was a blessing. These provided the basis for new public-health groups set up to combat AIDS and promote safer sex. In Peru, Mexico and Nicaragua the gay movement was central to the emergence of AIDS support and education groups.

In Brazil some gay groups joined with social workers, liberal clergy and people with AIDS to establish HIV/AIDS organisations. Where an organised gay base was lacking (as in much of Africa and the Indian subcontinent) it was much harder to take action against HIV. In some countries, the gay presence in AIDS organisations has had to be played down. It is not uncommon for basically gay-run AIDS organisations to receive government funding even in countries where homosexuality is outlawed.[5] But activists and outreach workers may find themselves targets of abuse and ill treatment, especially in countries where homosexuality is taboo and/or illegal.

In 2001 four AIDS activists belonging to the Naz Foundation were arrested in the Indian city of Lucknow. They were held for more than 40 days, beaten and refused bail. The four had been disseminating safer sex information in the city's parks and cruising grounds. Arif Jafar, a veteran activist who established one of the country's first gay groups, Friends India, was one of those arrested. They were charged on anti-sodomy and anti-obscenity laws. They were also charged with 'promoting homosexuality'. In supporting their charges police produced a replica penis used to demonstrate the proper use of condoms and claimed it was a sex toy. The magistrate called the activists 'a curse on society'.[6] In Jamaica too, AIDS outreach work has its risks. In December 2000 a nurse was detained for handing out condoms.[7]

The need for information about safer sex cannot be overstated. British writer and researcher Jeremy Seabrook found that on the Indian subcontinent: 'It is not uncommon for men to believe not only that sex with men is safe but also that the discharge of semen into the body makes them stronger and secure against infection.'[8] Health workers in Africa report similar beliefs that 'you can be cured of AIDS by having sex with a virgin'.

Poverty

Today it is clear that the spread of AIDS has more to do with poverty than with gay lifestyles. Look at the statistics: 22 million people have died from AIDS-related illnesses over the past 20 years, three million in 2001 alone. In that year, 40 million were infected; 28 million of those in sub-Saharan Africa. In Botswana 36 per cent of adults have the HIV virus, in South Africa 20 per cent. In South and South-East Asia 6 million have HIV/ AIDS. This compares with 0.9 million in North America and 0.5 million in Western Europe.[9]

AIDS/HIV infection reflects social injustice. The poorest, most disadvantaged and least well nourished are most vulnerable to getting infected if they come into contact with the virus, and they have least access to treatment for its symptoms. They do not all live in the South. African Americans were 12 per cent of the US population but 47 per cent of new AIDS cases in 2000. African American and Hispanic women made up 25 per cent of the female population but 81 per cent of all US AIDS cases in 1999.[10] Moreover, poverty can drive women and men into risky commercial sex work which boosts the spread of HIV. In Thailand a girl can make 25 times more as a prostitute than by working in a textile factory.

Some transgendered people may also engage in more risky commercial sex in order to raise money for operations and other gender realignment therapies. The receptive party is always more vulnerable to HIV-infection than the penetrating partner and post-operative male-to-female transgendered sex workers are especially vulnerable, more so than their born-female counterparts.[11]

In either case getting the more powerful person – the client or the husband or the boyfriend – to wear a condom may be difficult, especially in strongly patriarchal societies.

Taking on Big Pharma

Today whether or not you can survive with AIDS, and for how long, depends upon power and money. The battle lines are clearly drawn between the poor who form the majority of the world's people and the rich multinational drug companies and their shareholders.

AIDS activists are targeting two areas of injustice: patents and unfair pricing of life-prolonging anti-retroviral drugs. For example, a daily dose of a Pfizer-patent drug in the US costs $12.30; in much poorer Guatemala it is $27.60. In India, however, a non-patented copy of the drug is available at just $0.64. In Brazil the government broke Hoffmann-La Roche and Merck patents by launching a programme to manufacture its own generic AIDS drugs. The anti-retrovirals were provided, for free, to 110,000 registered HIV-patients. The results were undeniable. AIDS deaths fell by half and Brazil has saved $677 million on treatment costs from 1997 to 2000.[12] Hoffman-La Roche and Merck complained to the World Trade Organisation. But Brazil stood firm. What's more the UN Commission on Human Rights and the World Health Organisation have backed Brazilian-sponsored motions supporting access to life-saving drugs as a basic human right.[13]

Cross-fertilisation of ideas and strategies between activists in countries of the South has been vital in fighting for the human rights of people with HIV. Mathew Damane, an HIV-positive South African, was among activists who (in defiance of drug patent laws) went to Brazil to bring back anti-retrovirals for fellow sufferers at home who could not get the drugs. 'Because I have been helped so much with this medication, I wish I could share it with all the others in South Africa.'[14] In Thailand too there have been victories for people with HIV/AIDS. In October 2002 the Thai Central Intellectual Property and International Trade Court ruled in favour of stripping the US drug company Bristol Myers Squibb, which had been acting illegally, of its exclusive right to manufacture the AIDS drug Videx in Thailand. 'At every step we have had to fight for treatment access and fight for the right to live,' says Paisan Tan-Ud, founding chair of the Thai Network of people living with HIV/AIDS, an organisation involved in the court battle:

'We have exposed the killing greed of the drug companies. We have exposed their illegal activities, and we will continue to fight until access is a reality for all people living with HIV in Thailand.' [15]

See also: Faith **and** Homophobia

Q

Queer

'We're here. We're queer. Get used to it!'
Queer chant.

● ● ●

'Queer' was a very common term of abuse for homosexuals during much of the 20th century.

Historian Rictor Norton has traced historically the colloquial uses of the word 'queer' and finds it common in the early 18th century in phrases such as 'queer-ken' (prison house), 'queer booze' (bad drink), 'queer bird' (a man recently out of prison); and 'queer cul' (a fop or fool – used concurrently with 'molly cull' a homosexual). It was not until the early part of the 20th century that the use of 'queer' to signify homosexual became established. According to Norton, it originated in the gay sub-culture of the times and only later became a mainstream derogatory term.[1]

During the 1990s the term was rudely reclaimed by homosexuals and others with the eruption of Queer Politics. Queer was radical. While identity politics depended on distinctions and definitions, queer politics had no truck with any of that. Anyone who challenged the dominance of straight life and straight norms counted as 'queer'. You didn't have to be either lesbian or gay to be queer. Bisexuals were queer, transsexuals were queer, even straights who passed as gay were queer. All identities could merge into a general 'queerness'. As an anonymous leaflet 'Queer Power Now' distributed on the streets of London in 1991 robustly manifested:

'Queer means to fuck with gender. There are straight queers, bi-

*queers, tranny queers, lez queers, fag queers, SM queers, fisting
queers in every single street in this apathethic country of ours.'2*

Queer Theory got its intellectual inspiration from a mixture of
postmodernism, feminism and the ideas of gay French historian
Michael Foucault. He saw homosexuality as a 'strategically situated
marginal position' from where it might be possible to glimpse and
devise new ways of relating to oneself and others. Queer politics
rejected gender oppression but valued its marginal, outsider
perspective. Cherry Smith described it this way:
*'Both in culture and politics, queer articulates a radical questioning
of social and cultural norms, notions of gender, reproductive
sexuality and the family. We are beginning to realize how much of
our history and ideologies operate on a homo-hetero opposition,
constantly privileging the hetero perspective as normative, positing
the homo perspective as bad and annihilating the spectrum of
sexualities that exists.'3*

Some welcomed the reclaimed 'Q' word with open arms. Filmmaker
Derek Jarman (who was interviewed wearing a T-shirt reading 'Queer
as Fuck') commented:
*'I never liked the word 'gay' (although I never said so) because it
exuded a false optimism. It wasn't my word. I was in the party of
miserabilists.'4*

Others weren't so sure. Harriet Wistrich commented: 'I don't use that
term. I associate it with gay men and I'm dubious about reclaiming
derogatory terms. The "queer agenda" as you call it isn't my
struggle.'5
    Queer activism has sometimes been at odds with the lesbian and
gay movement's civil rights approach. Whereas gay civil rights
strategists stress the unthreatening 'normality' of gay relationships as
part of the argument for equal rights, the Queer approach is more
oppositional and anti-assimilationist. The former strives for the right
to be accepted as normal, the latter for the right to be different.
'Queer asserts in-your-face difference,' writes sociologist Joshua
Gamson. 'Queer does not so much rebel against outsider status, it
revels in it.'6
    Actions have included mass, pan-sexual kiss-ins, especially at
events where political or religious homophobes may be speaking. The

 Queer politics? LGBT march in Cape Town, South Africa, 1993

© Eric Miller/Panos Pictures

main activist motor was Queer Nation – a typically anarchic, decentralised movement with no single unified theory or agenda. It had its origins in the US, but offshoots in Britain, Australia and other parts of Europe. There are also various groups involved in 'Queeruption' activities as part of the anti-globalisation movement that burst onto the streets of Seattle, Prague, London and Genoa.

The ultimate challenge of Queer politics is perhaps the way in which it questions the unity, stability and political utility of sexual and gender identities. It reminds us that labels and categories can easily become part of oppression. Its inclusiveness has been welcomed by many bisexual and transgendered people who were never at ease with lesbian and gay labels. Whatever response it gets, 'queer' is probably here to stay – well, for a while longer, anyway.

See also Diversity, Stonewall, Bisexuality and Trans Liberation

R

Rainbow flag

'Somewhere over the rainbow
Skies are blue
And the dreams that you dare to dream
Really do come true'
Judy Garland in *The Wizard of Oz*[1]

The rainbow, holding together all the colours of the world, is a potent symbol.

In the 1970s Civil Rights activist Jesse Jackson led the Rainbow Coalition in the United States. This social and political movement was dedicated to honouring diversity, including that of LGBT people. The rainbow also became – and still is – a symbol for the peace movement. The gates at Greenham Common airbase in the UK were named after the colours of the rainbow by peace campers during the 1980s. In South Africa the symbol became associated with the anti-apartheid struggle's desire to create a 'Rainbow Nation' whose multiracial agenda included freedom from persecution on the grounds of gender and sexuality as well as race.

Since the 1938 film *The Wizard of Oz*, gay men in particular have linked the rainbow to the magical world of Oz, located 'over the rainbow' and offering freedom from oppression and delight in companionship. But long before that, connections were made between the rainbow and sex or sexuality. In medieval and renaissance France it was believed that a person could 'change sex

• A gay couple kiss behind a rainbow flag during a rally of gay groups in Rio de Janeiro (August 2003). Gay groups in Brazil sharply criticised a Vatican document which condemned gay marriages as 'deviant'.

while passing under a rainbow'. In the Yoruba religion of West Africa and the African diaspora, the deity of the rainbow, Oshumaré, is an androgynous link between the world of mortals and that of the gods. In Brazil, Oshumaré is seen as the patron of gender variant, transgendered, gay, lesbian and bisexual people.[2]

From 1978 the rainbow acquired a specific meaning for those involved in the gay liberation movement. At that time San Francisco artist Gilbert Baker responded to a gay community request for a symbol, by creating a flag with eight stripes: pink, red, orange, yellow, green, blue, indigo, and violet. According to Baker, those colours represented, respectively: sexuality, life, healing, sun, nature, art, harmony, and spirit. Unfortunately, Baker had hand-dyed all the colours, and since the colour 'hot pink' was not commercially available, mass production of his eight-striped version became impossible. The flag was thus reduced to seven stripes.

In November 1978, San Francisco's gay community was stunned when the city's first openly gay supervisor, Harvey Milk, was assassinated. Wishing to demonstrate the gay community's strength and solidarity in the aftermath of this tragedy, the 1979 Pride Parade Committee decided to use Baker's flag. The committee eliminated the indigo stripe so they could divide the colours evenly along the parade route: three colours on one side of the street and three on the other. Soon the six colours were incorporated into a six-striped version that became popularised and that, today, is recognised by the International Congress of Flag Makers.[3]

In the 1990s the rainbow flag was adopted as an international symbol in the struggle for LGBT liberation. From Hong Kong to Mexico, it now appears in protests and parades around the globe. Namibia's LGBT rights organisation is called the Rainbow Project. The flag evokes the rich diversity of LGBT people around the world – a diversity held together by a common search for human rights.

In recent years the LGBT movement has been forming new coalitions, keeping alive the political spirit of the rainbow. Ecuador's LGBT and HIV/AIDS movements joined forces with indigenous rights groups in the late 1990s to oppose the government of the now deposed Jamal Mahoud. Together they campaigned successfully for a rewriting of the Constitution to enshrine human rights and anti-discrimination clauses on the grounds of race, sexuality and gender. Meanwhile, the mainly indigenous Mayan Zapatista movement in Mexico is the most LGBT-friendly and supportive of all political groups in the country. While in Argentina the Mothers of the Plaza de Mayo (the famous 'mothers of the disappeared'), chained themselves to the stairs of the Palace of Justice in Buenos Aires to protest police killings of transsexuals in the city.

See also Zapatistas and Stonewall

S

Stonewall

'We weren't taking any more of this shit. We had done so much for other movements. It was time... I remember when someone threw a molotov cocktail, I thought: "My God, the revolution is here! The revolution is finally here."'
Sylvia Rivera, on the Stonewall riots, July 1969[1]

• • •

On a hot, muggy summer's night on the 28 July, 1969 a New York, Greenwich Village gay bar hit the headlines and became a world-famous icon. Picture the scene: the Stonewall is heaving with gay men, lesbians and drag queens in all their finery. Suddenly, at about 1 am, the lights flash. People stop dancing: it's a police raid. The Morals Squad are back. The customers are led out and 'cattled' up against the police vans. They are pushed up against grates and fences. This is not an unusual occurrence. But tonight, instead of going obediently into the waiting police vans, some people start throwing coins. Then bottles. The Stonewall's customers are resisting. There are shouts of 'gay power'. Surprised police barricade themselves into the building. It's the first time anything quite like this has happened. They call for reinforcements. Protesters rip up a parking meter and begin to ram the door.

For many who were there, like transsexual Sylvia Rivera, it was a heady, unforgettable moment – and perhaps less of a complete surprise than it might have been for the police. She says:
'I always believed we'd fight back. I knew we would fight back. I just

101

didn't know it would be that night.'[2]

The protests continued for several nights running, and were followed by further protests and marches.

The 'Stonewall Riots' are often seen as the ignition point – the Boston Tea Party of the Gay Liberation movement in the West. Indeed they are charged with an almost sacred significance in gay history. But this was not really the first event of its kind. Paris and Amsterdam had seen similar outbursts in the previous year.

It was, perhaps, to be expected. The 1960s had been a decade of radicalism. The influence of the Black Civil Rights movement was tremendous – as became that of the Women's Movement a few years later. As black activists fought racism under slogans such as 'Black is Beautiful' and feminists examined and challenged sexism and proclaimed 'Sisterhood is Powerful', it was, indeed time to challenge the prejudice against homosexuals. Time for a slogan that went: 'Gay is Good.'

Joan Nestle remembers the Stonewall Inn before the riots:

'The cops would come in to check their nets, get their payoffs, joke with the men who stood by the door. They would poke their heads into the back room to make sure we were not dancing together, a crime for which we could be arrested. Of course, the manager flashed the red light ten minutes before the cops arrived to warn us to play our parts. We did, sitting quietly at the square tables as the cops looked over. But if they had looked closer, they would have seen hands clenched under the tables, femmes holding onto the belts of their butches, saying through the touch of fingers: don't let their power, their swagger, their leer, goad you into battle.'[3]

But even these mid-20th century acts of rebellion by gays and lesbians did not come out of the blue. They had precursors. A century earlier Karl Heinrich Ulrichs, a German jurist and journalist, urged the repeal of all laws that criminalised same-sex activity. There were other pioneers such as Karoly Maria Kertbeny, John Addington Symonds, Edward Carpenter and writers Oscar Wilde and Radclyffe Hall.

Early gay militants at London's First Gay Liberation Front March, Trafalgar Square, August 1971

© Peter Bull

In terms of creating a movement, the German Magnus Hirschfeld was most instrumental. He set up the Institute for Sexual Science in Berlin, which was to become a source of information and inspiration for gay people internationally. His library contained 12,000 books, 35,000 photos and countless manuscripts – all destroyed by Nazi students on 6 May 1933.[4]

The clampdown on homosexuals both during and after the World War II provoked another wave of political activism. In the US the Daughters of Bilitis and the Mattachine Society organised lesbians and gay men for mutual support. These were known as 'homophile movements'. The Campaign for Homosexual Equality in Britain is an example of a pre-Stonewall campaigning group.

With the rise of more militant factions, gay liberation had a surge of energy from the late 1960s. The tiptoeing of the homophile movements was replaced by greater boldness as people 'came out of the closet'. Gay liberation was not to be won by élites speaking softly in the corridors of power, but by ordinary people taking to the streets and demanding decriminalisation and freedom. Public marches forced the issue onto heterosexual public consciousness, not only in North America, Australasia and Europe but also in countries of the

South, such as Mexico and Argentina.[5] Some of the most radical street protests for LGBT liberation are currently taking place in Asia and Latin America where violence against LGBT people, especially at the hands of police or right-wing paramilitary movements, is of continuing concern to human-rights groups. The spirit of Stonewall is alive and kicking in many parts of the world today.

See also **Kertbeny, Against nature, Out, Untermenschen and Love.**

Trans Liberation

T

'Many of the transvestites that are here today will probably spend
the night in police stations... but we will continue calling these
same stations so that they will not "disappear", we will continue
asking for human rights'

Activist Lohanna Berkins at a demonstration protesting about the murder of fellow
transvestite Nadia, who was arrested by Buenos Aires police, placed in a straightjacket
and beaten unconscious.[1]

Vanessa Lorena Ledesma was arrested on 11 February 2000. Five
days later she was dead. A police report said she had died of a cardiac
arrest. However the autopsy reportedly revealed that her body
showed signs of torture, including severe bruising to feet, arms, back
and shoulders, and indications that she had been beaten while
handcuffed. No one was arrested for her killing in the Argentinean
city of Cordoba. Proceedings against police officers were halted.

Exactly a year later, another transsexual, Vanessa Piedrabuena,
President of the United Transvestites Association of Cordoba, was
threatened by police after taking part in a demonstration calling for
a reopening of the investigation into Ledesma's death. Police forced
their way into her home and told her they did not want to see her on
the streets any more and that 'something's going to happen to you
that's worse than what happened to Vanessa Ledesma'.

Before they left, one of the police officers put his gun to her head.
Vanessa Piedrabuena reported the threats to the Police Internal

Transvestite potter Grayson Perry, aka 'Claire' (see Preface) with his wife Philippa and daughter Flo when he won the 2003 Turner Prize.

© Richard Mills

Affairs Division, but they are not known to have taken any action.[2]

In recent years human rights organisations have documented alarming levels of abuse including torture of transgender people in the Americas. Transphobic violence has been particularly bad in Argentina. Sixty-four transvestites were murdered between 1995 and 1997 in Buenos Aires alone. Transgender activist Diana Sacayan, who publicly denounced police harassment and abuse of transvestites, was arrested in the city of Don Bosco, Argentina, in February 2002 and charged with robbery. Sacayan reported being tortured by police and alleged that she was not arrested for robbery but for refusing to pay a bribe to local police.[3]

In other Latin American countries too the police are often the main suspects and the clear-up rate of transphobic crime is low. In Chile, only one of 24 anti-transgender murders known to have been committed between 2000 and 2002 has been solved by police, according to the transgender organisation TravesChile and the gay group Unified Sexual Minorities Movement.[4] In Venezuela transgender people continued to face unrelenting police harassment more than a year after the murder of transgender activist Dayana (José Luis Nieves) in July 2000, allegedly by police according to the 2002 *Human Rights Watch Report*. The Commander of Police in the Venezuelan state of Carabobo, where the murder took place, announced:

'Homosexuals and prostitutes are to be ruled by the police code. They cannot move freely in the streets.'

Mexico too has seen violent campaigns against trans people. Between 1991 and 1994, 12 sexual minority men, many of them transvestite sex workers, were killed in the city of Tuxtla Gutierrez in the state of Chiapas. Activists drew attention to other similar cases but police refused to follow up links and no one was brought to trial.[5]

Sexual as well as physical abuse of trans people is common. Those arrested may be stripped, beaten and forced to perform sexual acts. Transgender people are often attacked in ways that strike at key manifestations of their identity. For example, male-to-female trans people have been beaten on their cheekbones or breasts to burst their implants, sometimes causing the release of toxic substances with severe health consequences.[6]

Abuse of trans people is not restricted to Latin America. Transvestite communities in Istanbul, Turkey have reported repeated harassment by police using sexual and other forms of abuse.

What's it all about?
But what exactly is 'transgender'? And why are trans people so vulnerable to abuse?

Transgender is a broad church. It includes transvestites or cross-dressers – that is people who simply dress as the opposite sex. They may or may not be gay. It includes transsexuals – people who do not identify at all with their birth gender. Sometimes people who experience this are described as suffering from 'gender dysphoria' and the feeling that they have been 'born into the wrong body'. This may be the experience of some but not all transsexuals. Some transsexuals undergo medical treatment to alter their biological or 'birth' gender identity. This may involve hormone treatment or surgery or both. This used to be called a 'sex change' operation or therapy but is now more commonly termed 'sex reassignment'. Some transgender people may be intersexuals – people born with ambiguous genitalia or unusual chromosomes. Or they may be eunuchs, called *hijras* in India. In addition, many people are transgendered in the sense that they live their lives in a gender different to their biological sex but they have done nothing to alter their biology.

One thing all transgender people have in common is that they challenge conventional notions of gender – of male on the one side, female on the other.

It is estimated that today one in 12,000 people in the world is a male-to-female transsexual, and one in 30,000 is a female-to-male transsexual. But the figure could be much higher when you take into account all the various ways in which a person might be trans.[7]

Transgender people are especially vulnerable in a number of ways – some of which bring them into unwelcome contact with the police and other authorities. They are discriminated against in employment: many lose their jobs once 'discovered' or once they start gender reassignment. Many more don't get jobs to start with, however well-qualified. A comparatively high number of male-to-female transsexuals become sex workers. This may be due to difficulties in getting other employment; it may also be a way of raising cash for operations. Sex work raises the risk of both HIV infection and violence. Yet using health services is often an ordeal for trans people, says US activist Leslie Feinberg. Reports of humiliation and worse are common. As a result many will avoid seeking medical help when they need it.[8] In several countries gender-reassignment operations are illegal. Some countries which allow surgery will not reissue documents in accordance with the new gender identity. This was the case in Britain until the law was changed in 2002. Parenting and access to their children is another area in which transgendered people are often denied their basic rights.

Legislation supporting transgender people
Increasingly governments – including those of states in Australia and the US and countries in the European Union – are introducing

'Let us always remember the friends and lovers who have to try and comprehend the change, as well as family members. It was easy to accept that someone was unhappy with an aspect of themself, and that they are moving down a path that will lead to their own happiness in the future, and anyone armed with the knowledge will have an easier time dealing.'
Karina, ex-lover of a transgendered teenager, Minnesota, US.[9]

legislation to ban discrimination against transgender people.

In 2002 New York adopted transgender anti-discrimination legislation, protecting all transsexual, transgendered and gender variant people from discrimination in housing, employment and public accommodation in five boroughs. At the UN six experts issued a joint statement urging lesbian, gay, bisexual and transgender activists to send them information regarding human rights violation based on sexual orientation or gender identity.

These advances are possible due to the work of a growing transgender movement headed by activists who are prepared to fight for their rights and challenge both the rigidity of the two gender model and the human rights abuses that arise from it. The two-sex system is not inevitable. It's just a product of societies hung up on reproduction, argues anthropologist Gilbert Herdt.[10] While many transsexuals will seek sex reassignment surgery, increasingly transsexuals are deciding against surgery – without feeling that they are compromising their core gender identity. More trans and intersex people are opting to live bi-gendered or hybrid-gendered lives, or choosing hermaphroditic bodies through surgery to match their core sense of who they are. Activist Michael Hernandez says:

'I have found a balance, a sense of peace. I am more than male and more than female. I am neither man nor woman, but a circle encompassing both... I just am. The name and the fit aren't that important any more... Gender and behaviour are as variable as the stars in the sky.'[11]

As political activism grows, and the sense of a transgender community develops, more are choosing the be 'out' as transgendered rather than 'pass' as one gender or another. Zachary I Nataf explains: 'As a transgendered man (female-to-male transsexual) I do not "pass" as simply male but am "out" to campaign for non-discrimination and Transgender Pride.'[12] Activist and writer Leslie Feinberg looks ahead:

'The women's liberation movement sparked a mass conversation about the systematic degradation, violence and discrimination that women faced in society... Now another movement is sweeping onto the stage of history: Trans Liberation. We are again raising questions about the societal treatment of people based on their sex and gender expression. This discussion will make new contributions to human consciousness.'[13]

See also: **Intersex, XXYY, and** Vegetarian sisterhoods.

Untermenschen
– or 'sub-human'

'The attraction of a man for a man signals the destruction of the State... if this vice continues to spread throughout Germany and we do nothing to combat it, it will mean the end of Germany, the end of the Germanic world.'
Heinrich Himmler, 1937.

In the 1920s Berlin had a flourishing gay culture. There were gay clubs and bars and the Institute of Sexology was known internationally for its progressive study of the nature of sexuality. It was the first organisation set up to promote the understanding and acceptance of homosexuality. In 1929 the Reichstag committee on the penal code recommended the abolition of Paragraph 175, by which male homosexuality had been a criminal offence throughout Germany since 1871. (As in British law, lesbianism was not mentioned.) This new move was the culmination of a 30-year campaign by Magnus Hirschfeld and his Scientific-Humanitarian Committee, and was supported by socialists, communists and many liberals and opposed by the parties of the right, especially the Nazis.

Nazi extermination of homosexuality
Then in 1933 the Nazis came to power. Hirschfeld's Institute of Sexology was ransacked and thousands of books and documents burned. Hirschfeld fled to France where he died in 1935.

The Nazis had made their position on homosexuality clear back in

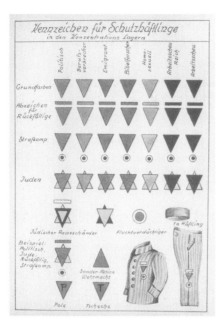

A chart of prisoner markings used in Nazi concentration camps. The horizontal categories list markings for the following types of prisoners: political, professional criminals, emigrants, Jehovah's Witnesses, homosexuals, workshy Germans, workshy of other nationalities. The vertical categories show the basic colours, then the markings for repeat offenders, prisoners in punishment kommandos, Jews, Jews who have violated racial laws by having sexual relations with Aryans, and Aryans who have violated racial laws by having sexual relations with Jews.

From US Holocaust Memorial Museum, courtesy of KZ Gedenkstaette Dachau

1928 when they announced: 'Those who are considering love between men or between women are our enemies.'[1] A purge followed. In 1935 the law against homosexuality was extended to any form of 'lewdness'. As little as a kiss or an embrace or even a fiction of homoerotic content was a criminal offence.[2] By the mid-1930s homosexuality was being declared depraved and homosexuals 'untermenschen' – which means 'sub-human'. Yet even the Nazi party had its fair share of homosexuals, including one of the 12 leaders, Ernst Rohm, and his band of followers. Rohm, a long-term friend of Hitler's, was nonetheless murdered on 30 June 1934 – the Night of the Long Knives.

Like Jews, Roma ('gypsies') and disabled people, homosexuals were seen as an obstacle to the Nazi project of 'improving' the human race by ensuring the reproductive supremacy of the Aryan race. Disabled people and those considered 'socially defective' were forcibly sterilised. While racial mixing might threaten the 'purity of the Aryan race', homosexuality, especially among Aryans, threatened its very survival.

From 1936 on, thousands of gay men, lesbians, transvestites and others were deported to concentration camps along with Jews, Roma and others labeled sub-human. A 22-year-old Austrian student, called Heinz Heger was among them. One day in 1939 there was a knock on the door of his family home in Vienna. It was the Gestapo, summoning him to their HQ. There he was interrogated and shown a picture of himself arm-in-arm with his 24-year-old boyfriend, Fred. Eventually Heger confessed. He was convicted, imprisoned, sent to Sachsenhausen then Flossenburg concentration camps where he remained until 1945 – one of the few homosexual inmates to survive. In his account, *The Men with the Pink Triangle*, Heger says:

'The prisoners' uniforms were marked with a coloured cloth triangle to mark their offence or origin... Jews, homosexuals and gypsies, the yellow, pink and brown triangles, were the prisoners who suffered most frequently and most severely for the tortures and blows of the SS and the Capos. They were described as the scum of humanity, who had no right to live on German soil and should be exterminated. Such were the oft-repeated words of the commandant and his SS subordinates. But the lowest of the low in this "scum" were we, the men with the pink triangles.'[3]

The general policy for gay inmates was to work them to death. Heger recalls:

'Our work then was as follows. In the morning we had to cart snow outside our block from the left-hand side of the road to the right side. In the afternoon we had to cart the same snow back from the right side to the left.'

But they were also subjected to medical experimentation:

'We who wore the pink triangle were prioritized for medical experiments, and these generally ended in death.'

Towards the end of 1943 a new instruction came from Himmler on the 'eradication of sexual degenerates'. He stipulated that any homosexual who agreed to be castrated and whose behaviour was good could be released from camp. Those who were released were sent to the Russian front to be butchered there. In 1944 a series of experiments aimed at the elimination of homosexuality were started at Buchenwald camp.

'In the fall of 1944... the Danish SS-Sturmbannfuhrer DR Vaernet appeared at Buchenwald concentration camp. With permission from Himmler... Vaernet started a series of experiments aimed at the elimination of homosexuality. The implantation of synthetic hormones into the right lower abdomen was meant to lead to a sex

drive reversal. Of the total 15 test subjects (including two previously castrated males)... two died, undoubtedly as a result of the operation... The others died a few weeks later as a result of general weakness...'.[4]

It is impossible to give an accurate figure for the total number of people killed by the Nazis on account of homosexuality. During the 12 years of Nazi rule 50,000 men were convicted for homosexuality and the majority of these ended up in concentration camps and did not survive. Large numbers of gay people were also sent to concentration camps without any legal proceedings and many were shot for homosexual offences within the armed forces.[5] One estimate suggests that 500,000 died in prisons or as result of medical experiments, summary executions and suicides provoked by persecution.[6]

And on it goes

What happened after the war is instructive. For gay survivors released in 1945 the injustice simply continued. After all, male homosexuality remained a crime in Germany for several more decades – as it was in the countries of liberating allies, the UK, Russia and the USA. As a result, the homosexual inmates of camps were not considered unjustly imprisoned. What's more they could be re-imprisoned. Compensation was a non-starter.

Heger, who owed his survival in the camps to the protection of an SS officer in exchange for sexual favours, had this experience after the war:

'My request for compensation for the years of concentration camp was rejected by our democratic authorities, for as a pink triangle prisoner, a homosexual, I have been condemned for a criminal offence, even if I have not harmed anyone. No restitution is given to "criminal" concentration camp victims.'

Nazi policies towards homosexuals were ignored and neglected by researchers. Little was published on the matter for several decades until an emerging gay rights movement in the 1970s 'discovered' the history of the Nazi persecution of homosexuals. In recent years more recognition has come. Israel was the first country officially to recognise gays as Holocaust victims. Memorials to gay Holocaust survivors have been put up in Amsterdam, Vienna and a number of other cities.

But others go on treating gay people as sub-human. The US group STRAIGHT (Society to Remove All Immoral Gross Homosexual Trash) has organised demonstrations celebrating the deaths of gay people from AIDS or from homophobic violence. Also in the US Christian Preacher Rev Fred Phelps advocates the death penalty for homosexuals. In Zimbabwe on 11 August, Heroes Day, 1995 President Mugabe told thousands of people who had gathered at Heroes Acre, the burial ground for fallen combatants, that homosexuals were 'worse than pigs and dogs'.[7] In Nepal teenagers Maya Tamang and Indira Rai were threatened by mobs in their village when their relationship was discovered. The girls declared that they loved each other. Neighbours described them as 'garbage that must be removed'.[8] In Moldova MP Vlad Cubreacov had this to say: *'To be homosexual doesn't only mean you are no longer father or mother, it means you are no longer a human being. They are people fallen before the face of God and the entire society.'*[9]

See also: **Clitoridectomy, Homophobia and Stonewall**

V.

Vegetarian sisterhoods,
Mother Clap and other queer histories

Andy Warhol... Johnny Ray...

William Burroughs... Jean Genet...

Isherwood... Wilde... Capote...

Auden... Jean Cocteau... Joe Orton

Add your name to this hall of fame

The answer is clear

They're All Of Them Queer

Add your name to this hall of fame

Stand up and cheer

They're All Of Them Queer

From *Those Legendary children* by Holly Johnson

Recovering 'queer history' – the stories of lesbian, gay, bisexual or transgender people in past eras – is not always easy. Records of sodomy trials in medieval Europe were often burned together with those convicted. Much subsequent evidence has also gone up in flames, thanks to fear and prejudice. Historians and biographers frequently find that evidence has been destroyed by friends and relatives, concerned to 'preserve the reputation' of sexual or gender non-conformists who have died. And if the history of gay men has been hidden, that of lesbians is doubly invisible – discriminated

An 18th century Indian illustration depicting women bathing together. Himachal Pradesh, India.

against on account of both sexuality and gender.

But queer history helps to make a connecting path through a heritage and experience that has all too often been silenced by prejudice. In 1953 beat poet Jack Spicer wrote: 'We homosexuals are the only minority group that completely lacks a vestige of a separate cultural heritage.'

Anthropological studies dating back several decades remained unpublished because the researchers feared damaging their own reputations. That has changed now thanks to scholars able and prepared to embark on the recovery of queer histories and traditions. For example, lesbian traditions have been found among rich Muslim women in Mombasa, Kenya; women-marrying-women customs in Ghana and Lesotho; same-sex relationships between cousins in Aboriginal Australian communities. And in China the 'vegetarian sisterhoods' described below.[1]

In some societies there was considerable cultural acceptance of sexual and gender diversity; in others people might create their own secluded communities or devise ways of living out their identities in secret. Here are a few examples of LGBT history through time and across the world:

China

During the 19th century, in the southern Chinese province of Guangdong, thousands of women entered relations with other women by forming sisterhoods. The women were mostly silk workers whose income allowed them some economic independence. They vowed to the Goddess Yin never to marry a man and formed sisterhoods with such names as 'The Golden Orchid Association' or the 'Association of Mutual Understanding'. The sisters lived together in co-operative houses and helped each other in cases of illness or death. Some houses were vegetarian halls where the eating of meat and heterosexual contacts were forbidden. In these houses women led a religious life, but not as strictly as in a Buddhist nunnery. Sexual relations between women occurred in the so called 'spinster halls'.

The sisterhoods were banned as feudal remnants after the victory of the Red Army in 1949 and many sisters fled to Malaysia, Singapore, Hong Kong and Taiwan.

But the tradition may not have died altogether. In 1987 anthropologist Saskia Wieringa conducted interviews with sisters living in a Buddhist temple in Singapore where the abbess and nuns talked freely of their sexual relations and described their choice to enter a 'vegetarian life' as a positive decision.[2]

Greece and Rome

So common was homosexuality and bisexuality in the culture of classical Greece that concerned teachers during prudish Victorian times were incapable of erasing all references. Famous gay Greeks included both the most influential philosopher, Socrates, and the most famous soldier, Alexander the Great. The Spartans allowed and even encouraged same-sex relations among women and men. Lyric poet Sappho who lived on the island of Lesbos gave her name (and that of her birthplace) to more than just a type of verse. In religious mythology, too, sexual diversity had its place: Zeus, that most powerful of deities, was portrayed hotly pursuing the beautiful youth, Ganymede. Some modern retellings of the old Greek stories are more coy. The 2004 Hollywood film *Troy* repackaged Achilles' lover Patroclus as his cousin.

More relaxed attitudes to sex and sexuality were also characteristics of ancient Rome. Prostitution, male, female, gay or straight, was legal. Male prostitutes would gain custom from both women and men. It was considered acceptable for male Roman citizens to penetrate but not be penetrated. However, Julius Caeser, rumoured to be bisexual, was described by one commentator as 'every woman's man and every man's woman'.[3]

France

At the beginning of the 13th century, Pope Innocent III decreed that convicted heretics should forfeit their property and be put to death. These edicts justified the bloody campaign to wipe out the Cathar (or Albigensian) heresy.

The Cathars, flourishing in southern France, taught that the body was physical and therefore evil. They did not accept the doctrine of resurrection or approve of the act of reproducing the body. Procreation only continued material pollution, and those engaged in sex ought to avoid procreation. Though high-ranking Cathars were celibate, others were not. Guibert de Nogent reported: 'men are known to lie with men, women with women.' The Cathars possessed some of the richest land in south-eastern France. The crusade against them in 1208 cost the lives of thousands. It ended a decade later when the last remaining Cathars committed suicide in their mountain stronghold of Montségur.[4]

Italy

Renaissance Europe saw both wide practice of homosexuality and extreme punishments for it. Michelangelo, Donatello and Leonardo da Vinci were all reputed to be gay, though they had to deny it to save their skins. Painter Gianantonio Bazzi was publicly known as Il

Sodoma ('The Sodomite'). Homosexuality was so common that special Officers of the Night were appointed to 'ensure peace and maintain good morals'. In Florence, Officers of the Night tried some 15,000 men and boys and convicted over 2,000 between 1432 and 1502. The convicted were pilloried, abused and beaten by righteous citizens. If they survived they would be burned at the stake. Youths under 14 who willingly submitted to homosexual advances were driven naked from the city.[5]

North America

In most Native American societies there were examples of same-sex marriages and transgender traditions, relating to both men and women. The European chroniclers who first came across these customs described them in terms that belonged to their own world, calling Native homosexual men 'berdache'. This was French for slave-boys and used to refer to receptive males. The name stuck – though its servile connotations were actually quite inappropriate. The term 'Two-Spirit' is now preferred.

In 1724 French Jesuit missionary Joseph Francois Lafitau condemned the berdaches for behaving like women, yet admitted this was not the Native American view: 'Their profession of this extraordinary life causes them to be regarded as people of a higher order, above the common man.' Gay transvestites were often shamans or healers of the tribe. Sometimes, because they seemed to combine male and female characteristics, they were given the role of mediating between the sexes.[6]

Islamic Mediterranean

Medieval Islam had a flourishing literature of homosexual eroticism. The 700 years of Moorish rule in Spain fostered far greater intellectual, religious and sexual tolerance than the Visigothic era that preceded it or the Christian one that followed. Poets of the Sufi tradition, in particular, focused on forms of transgendered and homo-erotic themes. This tradition inspired what is regarded as some of the most beautiful male love poetry in world literature, including the work of Jalal Al Din Rumi (1207-1273). There are a number of texts regarding homoerotic love influenced by Sufism. One such is Qabus-nama, who urges his son to fall in love and to be bisexual so that he can enjoy the love of other men as well as women.[7]

Japan

When the 16th century missionary Father Francis Xavier arrived in Japan he was shocked to encounter a great many Buddhist monks involved in sexual relationships with each other. He began to refer to homo-eroticism as 'the Japanese vice'. But the tradition was well-established in Japan and the Spanish priest did not get very far with his preachings against it. He reports: '...everything we tell them amuses them since they laugh about it and have no shame when they are reproached about so vile a sin.' Word got round, though. One report recounts how he and his missionaries were stoned by a gang of youths in the street yelling and jeering: 'So you're the ones who forbid sodomy!'[8]

Europe

There are many cases in 17th and 18th century Europe of women who dressed as men and passed themselves off as such. Some sought lives of adventure as soldiers or sailors; some wanted safety while travelling; and some did it to gain access to male power and freedom. Last but not least, some did it so that they might love and even marry other women. If the fraud were discovered it was not uncommon for these wives to claim not to know that their husbands were a little different from what might be expected. Women who cross-dressed could be severely punished – executed even. The main crime was not lesbianism as such, but fraud: for impersonating a man and assuming male social power. There were at least 119 cases in the Netherlands during the 17th and 18th centuries. One of the most infamous was Maria van Antwerpen, who had enlisted as a soldier and courted and married a woman. In February 1769 she was convicted in Gouda for 'gross and excessive fraud' and for 'mocking holy and human laws concerning marriage'. At her trial Maria argued that she was 'not like other women'.[9]

Britain

In 1720s London there were more homosexual pubs than in the 1950s. These 'molly houses', as they were called, ranged from private back rooms in gin shops to three-story public houses run by male couples. A thriving, almost entirely working-class, gay subculture centred around such establishments, where irreverent rituals would take place, such as a 'mock births' (the baby's part played by a cheese) or 'wedding nights' (sometimes involving a mock chaplain). Many of the men dressed in drag and adopted female names. Margaret Clap (known as Mother Clap) ran one of the most popular pubs. Customers would come from miles around, especially on Sunday nights. Her house had been under surveillance for two years when, with the help of the puritanical Societies for Reformation of Manners, it was raided by police in 1726. Mother Clap was found guilty of keeping a disorderly house in which she procured and encouraged persons to commit sodomy. It is uncertain that she survived the vicious pillorying she received. Of the 40 'mollies' arrested, three were hanged. A wave of popular outrage during the next 10 years led to more hanging and pillorying. The hanging of men for being gay was to continue into the 19th century.[10]

Africa

Among the Azande people living in south-western Sudan, northern DR Congo, and the south-eastern corner of the Central African Republic, a form of intergenerational homo-eroticism was practised long before the arrival of Europeans and until the beginning of the 20th century, according to anthropologist Edward Evans Pritchard. Often the relationship was between a warrior and a younger male, but Azande women too had sex with each other. This was somewhat feared by men as it was thought to double a woman's power. Love-making between women led to the birth of the 'cat people' it was believed. Lesbianism seems also to have been common among those who lived in the courts of princes in which a dildo fashioned from a root was used.

Transgendered homosexuality is documented among the Nuba people of Sudan. According to anthropologist SF Nadel: 'homosexuals... wear women's clothing, do women's work, and adopt women's ways.' Nadel also reports traditional same-sex marriages with transgendered 'wife' and 'husband' living together and 'keeping a common household'.

In several other African cultures – the Lango people of Uganda, Meru of Kenya, Ila of Southern Zambia, and Zulu people of South Africa – there is evidence of transgendered males acting as spiritual functionaries.[11]

See also: **Not in our culture**, **Homophobia** and **Marriage**

We are family

'There are kids who refuse to sit with me at lunch. They call me ugly. Some get right up in my face and call me a fag because I speak against homophobia. But I try to hold my head high because I know of plenty of other kids who have gay parents but who don't feel safe about coming out... I want to wear my rainbow so that they know someone else is out there.'[1]

Sol Kelley-Jones, a 'spokeskid' for gay rights, who at the age of 10 testified before a Wisconsin Legislative Committee on a bill prohibiting same-sex marriage. Her parents are lesbians who had been together for 20 years and she did not see why her family should not have the same rights as any other child's.[2]

The idea that lesbian or gay or transgendered people might enjoy equality with heterosexuals is often seen as a threat to 'the family', something that may even destroy it.

Anti-gay commentators, be they journalists, religious leaders or politicians, almost invariably slip the emotive 'F' word into their arguments. In the United States groups dedicated to waging war on the 'homosexual agenda' have adopted names such as Focus on the Family and the Family Research Council. These groups believe that humankind exists to reproduce itself, which is the fundamental purpose of sex. They assert that the natural unit for reproduction is the heterosexual nuclear family. Homosexuality does not produce children. In their view it is therefore unnatural and a threat to the natural family. They claim that gay people undermine the family and family values and are therefore enemies of 'The Family'.

What gets lost in this kind of thinking is that LGBT people have families too. They are somebody's daughter or son or uncle or aunt or nephew or niece or cousin. And they may well be somebody's parent or even grandparent.

There are a great many lesbian, gay or transgender parents in the world today. As prejudices are gradually eroded in some parts of the world, and laws become less discriminatory, there are likely to be many more in the future. In Britain, Australia, the Netherlands and Canada same-sex partners may now foster and adopt children. More open-minded attitudes in relation to custody, rights for non-biological parents, and access to donor-insemination services, have in the course of just a few years made it easier for LGBT people who are, or want to be, parents. In other parts of the world the reality is still far from this.

'I would become a devil in people's minds'

Tendai lived with her husband and children in her parents house in Zimbabwe for five years. After a while she realised she was attracted to women and could no longer pretend otherwise. Through a friend in South Africa, she learned about GALZ, a gay and lesbian organisation in Zimbabwe. She became a member and started to receive the organisation's quarterly magazine. Her father found the magazines, got suspicious and pressed Tendai until she admitted she was 'one of them'. She was immediately thrown out of her family home and told never to come back. Her children were to remain with their father and for the next three years Tendai was denied any contact with them. 'It was so painful!' she says. 'But I can't change.'[3]

For Irena, a Russian lesbian, family and state conspired to break her bond with her child. This is in spite of the fact that homosexuality is not actually illegal in Russia:

'In 1995 Irena .... was ordered by her sisters to give up custody of her son and to get psychiatric treatment to "cure" her of her homosexuality. Her mother threatened to disclose Irena's sexual orientation to the authorities unless she comply. Two private investigators were hired by her parents. Claiming to have a video of Irena and her partner having sex, the investigators tried to blackmail the lesbian couple. When the latter went to the police to complain, the officer responded by sexually harassing them. The private investigators then abducted her at knifepoint and raped her. She did

● Thirteen-year-old Kylie Ahlers writes a letter to Massachusetts State Senate President Robert Travaglini. She and other children of gay and lesbian parents joined a protest by same-sex marriage supporters at the Massachusetts Statehouse (February, 2004). Kylie lives with her mother and her mother's lesbian partner, who say that they would marry for Kylie's benefit as soon as same sex partners are allowed to legally marry in the state. Senate President Travaglini refused to meet the children or their parents.

not report the rape to the police because of her previous experience at their hands...'

Irena finally gained asylum in the US.[4]

The recurring fears for LGBT parents, especially lesbians, is that they will lose their children, be thrown out of the family or community and become destitute as a result. Their best strategy is often to keep quiet. Ming, living in China, hides her relationship with her married female neighbour:

'There are no lesbians here! How can one be lesbian in this country? I married 10 years ago when I was 26; now I have a nine-year-old child. What can I do? If I "came out" to my husband and parents I would become a devil in people's minds, not so much because of my

tongxinglian [homosexuality], but for failing in my obligation and responsibility as a wife and daughter and mother.'[5]

Suitable parents

Those who oppose gay equality often claim that LGBT people are 'unsuitable' and that children will be damaged by the experience of being brought up by them. Lesbians are commonly accused of being too unstable, gay men too promiscuous. It is claimed that children of lesbians and gays will be confused in their gender-role identity. They will be 'corrupted' into becoming homosexual too. They will be rejected by society and unable to form normal social relationships.

But numerous research studies, mainly in the United States and Britain, have followed cases from childhood to adulthood and produced no evidence to support these claims. They found, in fact, that the children of lesbians and gays grew up pretty much as their counterparts in heterosexual households. One difference was that children in non-heterosexual households tended to be more open to the possibilities of different kinds of relationships. Even so, they were no more likely to be homosexual than the population as a whole.[6]

The main problem facing children of LGBT parents is prejudicial attitudes in society. Kate Mariat recounts this exchange with her then 11-year-old daughter:

'My younger daughter could not associate me, or other lesbians she had come to know and like, with the hatred and dismissal of lesbians she encountered at school and play. I can remember a peculiar conversation with her when she was in her first year of secondary school. She came in from playing and found me upstairs sorting clothes.

"I don't like lesbians."

"I'm a lesbian."

"I don't like lesbians."

"But you like... [I named some friends]."

"Ye-es," she paused. "I don't like lesbians."

And she went back out to play. When she read this passage we discussed whether or not I should include it. Sensitive though we are to it, it illustrates an important point. It was not that she didn't like lesbians, it was what other people thought of lesbians that made her feel bad.'[7]

Yet 'what other people think' can change – and can be changed. This 14-year-old British girl has an unusual family situation, yet finds support in the policy her school has adopted:

'I've actually got three Mums but I live between two households. There are lots of advantages because it means I got a wider range of life, and when I have a row, I can talk it through with one of my other mums. It's nice living with lesbians because it means you get to make choices about your own identity. All my friends like my Mums, and at school we have an equal opportunities policy about different families so there's no teasing or anything like that. The only drawback about living between two households is that sometimes I forget things...'[8]

In the West a generation – if not more – of children has been brought up with different families, creating a new way forward, just as loving and nurturing as the more traditional model. Until recently the focus has been mainly on lesbian parenting. But the desire of male couples to become fathers is becoming more common. Sometimes lesbian and gay couples get together to parent children – this is easier in places with a large lesbian and gay community. But there are other ways. In a highly publicised case in 1999 British gay couple Barrie Drewitt and Tony Barlow had twins in an arrangement with a surrogate mother in the US, and won a landmark legal battle to keep the children.

In December 1999 the European Court and Commission on Human Rights found that Portugal was in breach of Article 8 – the right to privacy – in a case where a Portuguese man lost custody of his child on the grounds of homosexuality and was granted access only on condition that he hide his orientation. This was a significant victory in getting the European Court at last to recognise the rights of lesbian and gay families. But for thousands of LGBT people living in countries where homosexuality is still a crime, or where social attitudes are violently hostile, such families remain a distant dream.

See also: **Judges, Marriage, Homophobia and Youth.**

X
● ●

XXYY

'What makes a man a man – testosterone? What makes a woman a woman – oestrogen? If so, you could buy your gender over the counter at any pharmacy.'
Kate Bornstein[1]

● ● ●

A child is born. 'Boy or girl?' tends to be the first question asked. We are culturally conditioned to be acutely conscious of gender. More than this, we automatically classify people in a binary way – male or female – that allows little room for ambiguity.

But actually ambiguity is coded deep into our biology. We begin life in the womb with a common anatomy. It becomes different if there is a Y (male) chromosome present. This activates the production of testosterone, the relevant receptors in the brain, and the formation of testes. The other features that do not develop remain in the body in vestigial form. Usually XX equals female, XY equals male. But there are other sets of gender chromosomes that may also commonly occur, such as XXY, XXX, YYY, and XO.[2]

Other factors that need to be taken into account apart from chromosomes include: hormones (oestrogen and testosterone); gonads (ovaries and testes); genitals (vagina and penis); reproductive capacities (sperm-carrying and inseminating; gestating and lactating); and internal organs such as the uterus or prostrate. These factors are not always consistent with each other.

Boy, girl, or ?? Gender verification proved problematic when women athletes started being subjected to it by the International Olympics Committee. From 1966 female competitors had to undergo degrading medical examinations. In 1968, genetic sex testing was introduced – but this failed to deal with ambiguous hereditary conditions. An early victim of this testing, highly traumatic for the athlete, was Polish sprinter Eva Klobukowska, who had previously passed gynaecological examinations but when sex chromatin testing was introduced was found to have one chromosome too many to be declared a woman. Her rare XXY condition gave her no advantage over other athletes, but she was forced to return her Olympic and other medals in a glare of publicity. This testing showed that sexual identity can be complicated: some XX individuals are not really females and some XY athletes are physiologically females.

What is gender?

How would you know if you are 100 per cent female or 100 per cent male, chromosomally or hormonally? Most of us need never find out, because there are few occasions in everyday life when our gender would need to be tested.

If we wanted to take part in the Olympic games we would have to take chromosomal sex tests. But other sports bodies have abandoned these. The British Journal of Sports Medicine claims that one in 500 athletes would fail a chromosome test. This is because physical appearance is not necessarily affected by chromosome variations. A test might determine that an athlete is not a woman for the sake of competition – but that wouldn't make her a man in everyday life. Even the ability to reproduce is not a clear indicator: some intersexuals have had children. All considered, the biological line between male and female is fuzzy.[3]

So what is gender? For some, like writer Jan Morris, herself a male-to-female transsexual, it is something almost spiritual. She describes it this in her book *Conundrum*, which marked her journey from male to female:

'That my conundrum might simply be a matter of penis or vagina, testicle or womb, seems to me still a contradiction in terms, for it concerned not my apparatus, but myself... To me gender is not physical at all, but is altogether insubstantial... It is the soul perhaps... It is essentialness of oneself, the psyche, the fragment of unity'.[4]

Her views are not dissimilar to the traditional Native American Two Spirit (or 'Berdache') saying: 'You are what you feel. You are what your dreams make you...'[5] For others, gender is emphatically physical. This is Lou Sullivan:

'The female-to-male experiences a male body every single day of her life. Through strong engulfing fantasy, she "feels" her broad shoulders, "feels" her flat chest, her low voice. She feels the need to carry more bulk between her legs and may wear padding. With this self image, she is met in the mirror every single day of her life by someone she doesn't recognize.'[6]

Most people, who are not transgender or transsexual or intersexual, rarely have to question their own gender or think about what their gender might mean. When British writer Will Self was asked to write the text for *Perfidious Man*, a photo-book on masculinity, he was –

unusually – lost for words. Then he had an idea. He would have as his main focus a man who very consciously knew what masculinity was: Stephen Whittle, a prominent female-to-male transgender activist.

Gender as social control

Perhaps the most important consideration when thinking about gender is not biology or psychology or spirituality, but how the idea of gender is used as tool of social control. Women have always experienced this, to varying degrees. In many countries of the world your gender can determine all your rights: your right to political power, property, employment, to drive a car, to show your face in public, to keep your own children, even your right over your own body. People who stray from gender norms are punished in a world dominated by patriarchy.

Under the mundane conventions of gender-tyranny men are supposed to behave 'like men' and women 'like women'. Those who transgress from these norms are likely to be met with unease, disapproval or punishment. Much anti-gay sentiment or homophobia has to do with infringing these gender rules or conventions. It is no accident that gay men who display traits considered to be 'effeminate' and lesbians who come across 'masculine' are far more likely to be victims of homophobic violence and discrimination than those who adhere more closely to normative gender conventions.

Indeed, many of the original proscriptions against homosexuality were couched in terms of men behaving 'in a womanish fashion'. And in some cultures, especially in Latin America, it is considered that only the receptive male partner is a real homosexual. The penetrative partner is just 'doing what a man does'.

As homosexuality becomes gradually more acceptable in many parts of the world, transgender still seems to provoke deep unease. Much of the violence against LBGT people is directed towards transgender people, especially in Brazil, Argentina and Colombia. These may be transvestites (men who dress 'as women', or women 'as men') and/or transsexuals (people who do not identify with the biological gender they were born into). Today transgender presents a radical challenge to the convention of seeing a person in terms of their gender rather than as, first and foremost, a human being.

See also: Intersex **and** Trans Liberation

131

Y
● ●

Youth

'To be a gay kid, there was this internal process you are going through. Everything you see around you is not like you. Your parents are not like you. The commercials you see on TV aren't like you. Your friends aren't like you... And on top of that, if you are harassed in school...'

Derek Henkle, who as a teenager started a court case against his former Nevada, US, school for allowing persistent homophobic bullying.[1]

● ● ●

Children, it is said, need protecting from homosexuals. Back in 1928, James Douglas, editor of the *Sunday Express*, wrote about the lesbian novel *The Well of Loneliness* that 'I would rather give a healthy boy or healthy girl a phial of prussic acid than this novel.'[2] More recently, Robert Knight of the US anti-gay Family Research Council has said: 'Homosexuals say they don't want children, but boy they put a lot of energy into going after them.'[1]

Paedophilia and homosexuality are inextricably linked in the minds of many people – in spite of lack of convincing evidence to show that children are at greater risk from homosexual adults. Statistics suggest the contrary: the majority of people who sexually abuse children are male and the majority of children who are sexually abused or exploited are female.

But fear of homosexuality's impact on children is widespread and has unfairly jeopardised the careers of many lesbian and gay people working with young people. It has militated against lesbian and gay parents in custody cases. For example, Portugal's Tribunal de Relacao stated in 1996: '[Homosexuality] is an abnormality and children should not grow up in the shadow of abnormal situations; such are the dictates of human nature.'[3] Such attitudes have also led to laws banning 'the promotion' of homosexuality in schools by presenting gay lifestyles as acceptable and a normal part of life.

The greatest damage of all, however, is done to children and teenagers themselves – especially those who may be lesbian or gay or transgendered.

Always a lonely boy

You were the one

That they'd talk about around town

As they put you down

And as hard as they would try

They'd hurt to make you cry

But you'd never cry to them

Just to your soul

No you'd never cry to them

Just to your soul

Bronski Beat, *Small town boy*

Youth in peril

The organisation Human Rights Watch documents an alarming number of attacks against lesbian, gay, bisexual and transgender school students around the world. Most occur at the hands of fellow students or pupils but in some cases staff are directly responsible.

Take the experience of US schoolboy Derek Henkle. When word got round that he was gay, his classmates subjected him to a daily routine of bullying which involved calling him names, spitting at him and pelting him with food. Then one day:

'I was in the middle of the parking lot of my school and a group of [boys] surrounded me. They said "let's string up the fag and tie him to the back of the truck and drag him down the highway". They took a lasso out and started throwing it around my neck... All I can remember is being surrounded by these people and how scared I was, scared to death for my life.'[4]

Brandon Teena (left) with girlfriend Lana Tisdel. Brandon was born a girl but lived as a boy until two male friends discovered his birth gender and killed him.

AP Photo/Bless Productions

Distressed and hysterical, Derek found a school vice-principal and told her what was happening to him. She laughed and told to 'be more discreet' about his homosexuality. The teachers made no attempt to confront the bullies. Eventually it was decided to move the teenager to another school, but the same thing happened there and he had to move again. After several more moves, Derek left school altogether, aged 16, without finishing his studies.

Pervasive homophobia, whether or not it leads to violence, creates a climate of fear which can disrupt learning or even rob LGBT people of their right to an education. It can also push young people to the brink of suicide.

One gay youth was at school in his native Syria in 1994 when a teacher held him back after class and raped him, accusing him of being 'a sin to this world'. The boy moved to Jordan where, five years later, he was sexually assaulted again. When he informed the police they refused to take him seriously and threatened to put him 'somewhere scary' if he bothered them again. Like many young and isolated LGBT people facing daily hostility, he became suicidal. Finally he decided to tell his parents about his sexual orientation. 'My father became enraged and started hitting and kicking me, saying I was degrading the family name... [he] threw me out on the street.' The boy became increasingly desperate. Eventually he began to search for information about LGBT organisations in the Middle East and in other regions. This information finally led him to apply for asylum in the US, which was granted in the year 2000.[5]

For 'their own good'

Crossing the gender line can be as perilous as being gay – even more so in some societies. In the US Midwest where teenager Brandon Teena grew up, girls are girls and boys are boys and those who blur the two do so at their peril.

Brandon Teena was born as a girl but lived and successfully 'passed' as a boy, moving from town to town and even having heterosexual girlfriends. But when Teena's birth gender was discovered by local youths he had befriended, they were furious. They brutally beat and raped him. Police failed to arrest Teena's assailants, who were able to track their victim down and kill him. Teena's story was featured in the film *Boys Don't Cry*.

It is not uncommon for communities or even family members to mete out fierce punishment to youngsters who do not follow the 'correct' gender path. Such violence is often justified as being for the young person's 'own good'. Rape is used in a similar way, especially against teenage girls who show no interest in getting married. This account comes from a girl in Zimbabwe. It took place in her family home – and under her parents' orders:

'They locked me in a room and brought him everyday to rape me so I would fall pregnant and be forced to marry him. They did this to me until I was pregnant.'[6]

Nor is it uncommon for male rape to be used to punish boys suspected of being gay. Serkan Altan reports from Turkey:

'Any boy aged eight years or older who displays any hint of effeminacy is very likely to be raped. Then the torture starts, especially in school. We homosexuals learn in school, along with other things, that we are going to be raped, beaten and tortured by the public and police.'[7]

Youth resistance

Resistance to these forms of violence and injustice is coming from many quarters – not least from young people themselves. In January 2000, Derek Henkle, the US teenager mentioned above, brought a civil-rights action against education officials in Nevada claiming that they had repeatedly and wilfully failed to take action against continuous and severe ill treatment. He won his case and was awarded over $400,000 in a landmark ruling in 2002.[8]

In Colombia two students, Pablo Enrique Torres Gutierrez and José Prieto Restrepo, took their church-run school to court for excluding them for being gay. The case was referred to the Colombian Supreme Court which in 1998 found in favour of the two boys.[9] In Britain teenager Ewan Sutherland brought a case to the European Court to challenge the unequal age of consent for gay men, which eventually led to the law being repealed.

There are many ways in which people are campaigning for justice and equality. They include getting LGBT issues included in the curriculum, pressing local authorities to adopt anti-discrimination legislation, making LGBT information available in schools and libraries, training teachers and administrators in diversity issues, and prohibiting discrimination in any public service institution.

In theory, the UN's Convention of the Rights of the Child provides strong protection to children against all forms of discrimination and violence. In practice, the Convention has rarely been invoked or used to benefit young LGBT people. There is, however, growing recognition of the harmful impact homophobia may have on a child's right to an education.

There's a long way to go – but increasingly young LGBT people and those campaigning for their rights are challenging the bullying, violence and injustice of homophobia. In the words of Derek Henkle: *'I am ready to go out there and change minds and attitudes. I am ready to go out there full force and say: "Come on! Let's all jump on... and let's ride to a place that's a much happier place than this".'*[10]

See also **We are family** and **Equality**

Z

Zapatistas

'We Zapatistas, men, women, and other, but still zapatistas, greet lesbians, gay, transsexual and bisexual dignity.

Long live your fighting spirit, and a different tomorrow, that is, one that is more just and human, for all those who are different.'

Subcomandante Insurgente Marcos, from the mountains of the Mexican south-east, Mexico, June 1999.[1]

Mexico's record on protecting and respecting its sexual minority people is not the finest. In the five-year period between 1995 and 2000, the Independent Civil Commission on Homophobic Hate Crimes recorded 199 murders of homosexuals, almost all of them unsolved. A commission member, Arturo Diaz, estimates that because of under-reporting – especially in the countryside – the death toll of gay men and women was actually closer to 500 in that period.[2]

Homophobic violence and police brutality have prompted a number of gay Mexicans to seek political asylum abroad. A 1999 report from the United Nations urged outgoing President Ernesto Zedillo to investigate the murders and make the protection of lesbians and gays a priority in the country.

But things have not improved under President Vicente Fox's conservative PAN government. Right-wing officials in PAN-run cities, often in conjunction with the Catholic Church, have been pushing for openly homophobic agendas. In the city of Cordoba in Veracruz, the PAN mayor launched a 'Clean Cordoba of Scum'

● Zapatista supporters on the march in Chiapas, southern Mexico, 1999.
Unusually for the Mexican political left, the Zapatista movement has taken up
lesbian and gay struggles.

© AP Photo/Eduardo Verdugo

crusade aimed specifically at sweeping gay sex-workers off the streets.

For Mexico's 'macho' political left, gay and lesbian rights have
never been high on the agenda either. There is one exception however:

the largely Mayan Indian Zapatista Army of National Liberation (EZLN). Since the earliest days of their rebellion the Zapatistas have embraced lesbian and gay struggles. They made a point of inviting gay and lesbian representatives to their meetings and festivals in the Lacandon jungle. In the words of Zapatista leader Subcomandante Marcos:

'What do lesbians, homosexuals, transsexuals and bisexuals have to be ashamed of? Let those who rob and kill with impunity be ashamed: the government! Let those who persecute the different be ashamed! Many [LGBT people] must conceal themselves – at times from themselves – but they do not for that reason renounce the right that belongs to every human being: that of respect of their dignity, without regard to the colour of their skin, their language, their income, their culture, their religious belief, their political ideology, their weight, their stature or their sexual preference.

For those who are present at this mobilization, our admiration for your courage and audacity to make yourselves seen and heard, for your proud, dignified and legitimate: "Ya Basta".'[3]

Ya Basta. That's enough. Enough injustice, enough abuse. It's a call that is echoing in many corners of the world today where people are finally saying 'no' to ancient, entrenched prejudices. It's a sentiment that in 2002 brought 400,000 people onto the streets of Sao Paulo to celebrate gay pride, setting a new world record. The city's mayor, Marta Suplicy, told the crowds of her pride at being a citizen of a place that could hold such an event. Her party, the Brazilian Workers' Party led by President Lula, has been for many years chipping away at the maschismo that often lies deep in South American political culture, be it of the left or the right. *Ya Basta* is also at the heart of the African National Congress's decision to include homophobia in its list of prejudices constitutionally unacceptable in the new South Africa. And it inspires attempts everywhere to create more tolerant and just societies that respect human dignity and feelings – from the Netherlands to the Philippines to the Bahamas.

See also: Homophobia **and** Rainbow

National legislation around the world on homosexual acts

This is not a definitive survey but a rough guide based largely on non-Amnesty International sources. In particular, it is not always clear whether legislation banning homosexual acts applies to women. In some countries, even when homosexual acts are legal, the state may encourage attacks on LGBT people, or fail to protect them from attack.

Afghanistan Illegal for men and women. Maximum penalty: death.

Albania Legal for men and women.

Algeria Illegal for men and women. Maximum penalty: three years' imprisonment or a fine.

Andorra Legal for men and women.

Angola Illegal for men and women.

Antigua and **Barbuda** Legal for men and women.

Argentina Legal for men and women.

Armenia Legal for men and women.

Aruba Legal for men and women.

Australia Legal for men and women.

Austria Legal for men and women.

Azerbaijan Legal for men and women.

Bahamas Legal for men and women.

Bahrain Illegal for men and women. Maximum penalty: 10 years' imprisonment.

Bangladesh Illegal for men and women. Maximum penalty: life imprisonment.

Barbados Illegal for men and women.

Belarus Legal for men and women.

Belgium Legal for men and women.

Belize Legal for men and women.

Benin Illegal for men and women.

Bermuda Legal for men and women.

Bhutan Illegal for men and women. Maximum penalty: life imprisonment.

Bolivia Legal for men and women.

Bosnia-Herzegovina Legal for men and women.

Botswana Illegal for men. Maximum penalty: seven years' imprisonment.

Brazil Legal for men and women.

Brunei Illegal for men and women. Maximum penalty: 10 years' imprisonment.

Bulgaria Legal for men and women.

Burkina Faso Legal for men and women.

Burundi Technically legal, but punishable as an 'immoral act'.

Cambodia Legal for men and women.

Cameroon Illegal for men and women.

Canada Legal for men and women.

Cape Verde Illegal for men and women.

Cayman Islands Legal for men and women.

Central African Republic Legal for men and women.

Chad Legal for men and women.

Chile Legal for men and women.

China Legal for men and women.

Colombia Legal for men and women.

Comoros Legal for men and women.

Congo Legal for men and women.

Cook Islands Illegal for men. Maximum penalty: 14 years' imprisonment.

Costa Rica Legal for men and women.

Croatia Legal for men and women.

Cuba Legal for men and women – but 'publicly manifested' homosexuality is punishable by up to one year's imprisonment.

Cyprus Legal for men and women.

Czech Republic Legal for men and women.

Democratic Republic of Congo Illegal for men and women.

Denmark Legal for men and women.

Djibouti Illegal for men and women.

Dominican Republic Legal for men and women.

Ecuador Legal for men and women.

Egypt Technically legal, but a variety of laws are used to repress gay men.

El Salvador Legal for men and women.

Equatorial Guinea No information.

Eritrea Legal for men and women.

Estonia Legal for men and women.

Ethiopia Illegal for men and women.
Maximum penalty: three years' imprisonment.

Finland Legal for men and women.

Fiji Illegal for men. Maximum penalty:
14 years' imprisonment.

France Legal for men and women.

French Guyana Legal for men and women.

Gabon Legal for men and women.

Gambia Illegal for men. Maximum penalty
14 years' imprisonment.

Georgia Legal for men and women.

Germany Legal for men and women.

Ghana Illegal for men.

Greece Legal for men and women.

Grenada Illegal for men.

Guatemala Legal for men and women.

Guinea Illegal for men and women.
Maximum penalty: three years or a fine.

Guinea Bissau Legal for men and women.

Guyana Illegal for men. Maximum penalty:
life imprisonment.

Haiti Legal for men and women.

Honduras Legal for men and women.

Hungary Legal for men and women.

Iceland Legal for men and women.

India Illegal for men and women.
Maximum penalty: life imprisonment.

Indonesia Legal for men and women.

Iran Illegal for men and women.
Maximum penalty: death.

Iraq Legal for men and women.

Ireland Legal for men and women.

Israel Legal for men and women.

Italy Legal for men and women.

Ivory Coast Legal for men and women.

Jamaica Illegal for men. Maximum penalty:
10 years' hard labour.

Japan Legal for men and women.

Jordan Legal for men and women.

Kazakstan Legal for men and women.

Kenya Illegal for men. Maximum penalty:
14 years' imprisonment.

Kuwait Illegal for men and women.
Maximum penalty: Seven years' imprisonment.

Kyrgyzstan Legal for men and women.

Laos Information not available, but arrests of
gays were reported in the 1990s.

Latvia Legal for men and women.

Lebanon Illegal for men and women.
Maximum penalty: One year's imprisonment.

Lesotho Legal for men and women.

Liberia Illegal for men and women.

Libya Illegal for men and women.
Maximum penalty: five years' imprisonment.

Liechtenstein Legal for men and women.

Lithuania Legal for men and women.

Luxembourg Legal for men and women.

Macedonia Legal for men and women.

Madagascar Legal for men and women.

Malawi Illegal for men and women.

Malaysia Illegal for men and women.
Maximum penalty: 20 years' imprisonment.

Maldives Illegal for men. Maximum penalty:
life imprisonment.

Mali Legal for men and women.

Malta Legal for men and women.

Marshall Islands Illegal for men.
Maximum penalty: 10 years' imprisonment.

Mauritania Illegal for men and women.
Maximum penalty: death.

Mauritius Illegal for men and women.
Maximum penalty: five years' imprisonment.

Mexico Legal for men and women.

Micronesia Legal for men and women.

Moldova Legal for men and women.

Mongolia Legal for men and women.

Morocco Illegal for men and women. Maximum
penalty: three years' imprisonment or a fine.

Mozambique Illegal for men. Maximum penalty:
three years' hard labour.

Myanmar Illegal for men and women.

Namibia Illegal for men.

Nauru Illegal for men and women.

Nepal Illegal for men and women.
Maximum penalty: life imprisonment.

Netherlands Legal for men and women.

New Zealand Legal for men and women.

Nicaragua Illegal for men and women.
Maximum penalty: three years' imprisonment.

Niger Legal for men and women.

Nigeria Illegal for men. Maximum penalty: death
(in states practising shari'a law).

Niue Illegal for men. Maximum penalty:
10 years' imprisonment.

North Korea No information available.

Norway Legal for men and women.

Oman Illegal for men and women. Maximum penalty: three years' imprisonment.

Pakistan Illegal for men and women. Maximum penalty: death.

Palestinian Authority Illegal for men and women. Maximum penalty: 10 years' imprisonment.

Panama Legal for men and women.

Papua New Guinea Illegal for men. Maximum penalty: 14 years' imprisonment.

Paraguay Legal for men and women.

Peru Legal for men and women.

Philippines Legal for men and women.

Poland Legal for men and women.

Portugal Legal for men and women.

Qatar Illegal for men and women. Maximum penalty: five years' imprisonment.

Romania Legal for men and women.

Russai Legal for men and women.

Rwanda Legal for men and women.

St Kitts and Nevis No information available.

St Lucia Illegal for men and women. Maximum penalty: 25 years.

Samoa Illegal for men and women. Maximum penalty: seven years' imprisonment.

Sao Tome and Principe Legal for men and women.

Saudi Arabia Illegal for men and women. Maximum penalty: death.

Senegal Illegal for men and women. Maximum penalty: Five years' imprisonment or a fine.

Serbia and Montenegro Legal for men and women.

Seychelles Illegal for men and women.

Sierra Leone Illegal for men and women.

Singapore Illegal for men and women. Maximum penalty: life imprisonment.

Slovakia Legal for men and women.

Solomon Islands Illegal for men and women. Maximum penalty: 14 years' imprisonment.

Somalia Illegal for men and women. Maximum penalty: three years' imprisonment.

South Africa Legal for men and women.

South Korea Legal for men and women.

Spain Legal for men and women.

Sri Lanka Illegal for men. Maximum penalty: 10 years' imprisonment.

Sudan Illegal for men and women. Maximum penalty: death.

Surinam Legal for men and women.

Swaziland Illegal for men and women. Maximum penalty: prison or fine.

Sweden Legal for men and women.

Switzerland Legal for men and women.

Syria Illegal for men and women. Maximum penalty: one year's imprisonment.

Taiwan Legal for men and women.

Tajikistan Legal for men and women.

Tanzania Illegal for men. Maximum penalty: 14 years' imprisonment.

Thailand Legal for men and women.

Togo Illegal for men and women. Maximum penalty three years' imprisonment.

Tokelau Illegal for men. Maximum penalty: 10 years' imprisonment.

Tonga Illegal for men. Maximum penalty: 10 years' imprisonment.

Trinidad and Tobago Illegal for men and women. Maximum penalty: 10 years' imprisonment.

Tunisia Illegal for men and women.

Turkey Legal for men and women.

Turkmenistan Legal position unclear.

Turks and Caicos Islands Legal for men and women.

Tuvalu Illegal for men. Maximum penalty: 14 years' imprisonment.

Uganda Illegal for men. Maximum penalty: life imprisonment.

United Arab Emirates Illegal for men and women. Maximum penalty: 14 years' imprisonment.

Uruguay Legal for men and women.

Ukraine Legal for men and women.

UK Legal for men and women.

USA Legal for men and women.

Uzbekistan Illegal for men. Maximum penalty: three years' imprisonment.

Vanuatu Legal for men and women.

Vatican City Legal for men and women.

Venezuela Legal for men and women.

Viet Nam Legal for men and women.

Yemen Illegal for men and women. Maximum penalty: death.

Zambia Illegal for men. Maximum penalty: 14 years' imprisonment.

Zimbabwe Illegal for men. Maximum penalty: three years' imprisonment.

Sources: www.sodomylaws.com, International Lesbian and Gay Association *World Legal Survey* on www.ilga.org, International Gay and Lesbian Human Rights Commission on www.iglhrc.org.

Endnotes

A

1 Amnesty International, *Crimes of hate, conspiracy of silence*, AI Publications. 2001.

2 *Ibid.*

3 Ian Sumner, Molengraft Institute for Private Law, Utrecht. Research for PhD thesis collected from Swiss Institute for Comparative Law, Lausanne. May 2003.

4 Byrne Fone, *Homophobia*, Metropolitan Books, New York. 2000.

5 Randy P Conner, David Hatfield Sparks and Mariya Sparks, *Cassell's Encyclopedia of Queer Myth, Symbol and Spirit*, Cassell, London and New York. Reprinted 1998.

6 Judith Mackay, *The Penguin Atlas of Human Sexual Behavior*, Penguin US. 2000.

7 Pat Caplan ed, The Cultural Construction of Sexuality, Tavistock Publications, London and New York. 1987.

8 Edward Carpenter in Havelock Ellis and John Addington Symonds, Sexual Inversion, Arno Press, New York. 1975, originally published 1897.

B

1 National Coalition for Gay, Lesbian, Bisexual and Transgendered Youth www.outproud.org.

2 Jeffrey Weeks, *Sexuality and its Discontents*, Routledge and Kegan Paul, London. 1985.

3 Kinsey, Pomeroy and Martin, 1948 and 1953, cited in Edward Stein, The Mismeasure of Desire: *The Science, Theory, and Ethics of Sexual Orientation*, Oxford University Press, Oxford and New York. 1999.

C

1 *Sunday Times*, 20 June 1999.

2 Richard Fitzgibbon, MD, NARTH website www.narth.com. 2003.

3 www.angelfire.com/ok2sxethic/homos[religioustolerance.org/hom]

4 www.geocities.com/davidmaus.beware.htm

5 Monika Reinfelder ed, *Amazon to Zami*, Cassell, London, 1999. Byrne Fone, *Homophobia*, Metropolitan Books, New York. 2000.

6 Martin Bauml Duberman, *Hidden from History: Reclaiming the Lesbian and Gay Past*, Penguin Books, London. 1991.

7 Don Romesberg, 'Thirteen Theories to "cure" Homosexuality' in Lynn Witt et al eds, *Out in All Directions: A Gay and Lesbian Almanac*, Warner Books. 1995.

8 *Ibid.*

9 Barry D Adam, Jan Willem Duyvendak and André Krouwel eds, *The Global Emergence of Lesbian and Gay Politics*, Temple University Press, Philadelphia. 1999.

10 Amnesty International, *Crimes of hate, conspiracy of silence*, AI Publications. 2001.

11 Don Romesberg, *op cit.*

12 Edward Stein, *The Mismeasure of Desire: The Science, Theory, and Ethics of Sexual Orientation*, Oxford University Press, Oxford and New York. 1999.

13 Human Rights Watch, *World Report 2002* www.hrw.org

14 Amnesty International, *op cit.*

D

1 Yik Hui, 'Living on the Fringes' in Bob Cant and Susan Hemmings eds, *Radical Records: 30 years of lesbian and gay history*, Routledge. 1988.

2 Peter A Jackson and Gerard Sullivan eds, *Lady Boys, Tom Boys, Rent Boys: Male and Female Homosexualities in Contemporary Thailand*, Harrington Park Press. 1999.

3 Evelyn Blackwood and Saskia Wieringa eds, *Female Desires*, Columbia University Press. 1999.

4 Jeremy Seabrook, 'It's what you do', *New Internationalist*, October 2000.

5 Evelyn Blackwood and Saskia Wieringa, *op cit.*

6 Peter Drucker ed, *Different Rainbows*, Gay Men's Press. 2000.

7 Kate More and Stephen Whittle, *Reclaiming Genders*, Cassell. 1999.

8 *Ibid.*

E

1 Quoted by Mark Gevisser, 'Mandela's Stepchildren' in Peter Drucker ed, *Different Rainbows*, Gay Men's Press. 2000.

2 Amnesty International news release, AI International Secretariat, 22 April 2003.

3 Andrew Osborn, 'Muslim alliance derails UN's gay rights resolution', *Guardian Unlimited*, 25 April 2003.

4 Ian Sumner, Molengraft Institute for Private Law, Utrecht. Research for PhD thesis collected from Swiss Institute for Comparative Law, Lausanne. May 2003.

5 Amnesty International news release, *op cit.*

6 International Lesbian and Gay Association www.ilga.org

7 Amnesty International, *Crimes of hate, conspiracy of silence,* AI Publications. 2001.

8 Amnesty International news release, *op cit.*

9 nternational Gay and Lesbian Human Rights Commission www.iglhrc.org

10 *Szivárvany, Juhasz and Palfry vs Hungary.* Ruling of the European Court of Human Rights.

11 South African News Agency SAFA in the BBC Summary of World Broadcasts, 3 August 1995.

12 PlanetOut, news roundup, 17 June 2003.

13 The Servicemembers Legal Defense Network (SLDN), *Conduct Unbecoming: Sixth annual report on 'Don't ask, don't tell, don't pursue, don't harass',* March 2000, www.sldn.org

F

1 Byrne Fone, Homophobia, Metropolitan. 2000.

2 Randy P Conner, David Hatfield Sparks, Mariya Sparks, *Cassell's Encyclopedia of Queer Myth, Symbols and Spirit,* Cassell. 1997.

3 BBC Radio 4, Today, August 2003.

4 Randy P Conner, David Hatfield Sparks, Mariya Sparks, *op cit.*

5 *Ibid.*

6 Anissa Helie, 'Holy hatred', *New Internationalist,* October 2000.

7 Martin Bauml Duberman, Martha Vicinus, George Chauncey eds, *Hidden from History.* Penguin 1991.

8 Anissa Helie, *op cit.*

9 Vanessa Baird, 'Taboo breakers', *New Internationalist,* October 2000.

10 Randy P Conner, David Hatfield Sparks, Mariya Sparks, *op cit.*

11 Vanessa Baird, *op cit.*

12 Randy P Conner, David Hatfield Sparks, Mariya Sparks, *op cit.*

13 Byrne Fone, *op cit.*

14 *Ibid.*

G

1 Edward Stein, *The Mismeasure of Desire: The Science, Theory, and Ethics of Sexual Orientation,* Oxford University Press, Oxford and New York. 1999.

2 Martin Bauml Duberman, Martha Vicinus, George Chauncey eds, *Hidden from History,* Penguin 1991.

3 ABC News, 22 April 1999.

4 Edward Stein, *op cit.*

H

1 Paul Cameron, 'Criminality, Social Disruption and Homosexuality', quoted by Mark E Pietzyk, *News Telegraph,* 10 March 1995 and www.hatecrime.org.

2 Byrne Fone, *Homophobia,* Metropolitan. 2000.

3 Vanessa Baird, 'Out South', *New Internationalist,* October 2000.

4 *Ibid.*

5 Rikki Beadle Blair, weblog, BBC Radio 4.

6 Phelps quotes by *State Press* (Arizona State University), 11 March 1998. Also on www.hatecrime.org.

7 www.hatecrime.org.

8 National Coalition for Gay, Lesbian, Bisexual and Transgendered Youth, www.outproud.org.

9 Byrne Fone, *op cit,* and Audre Lorde, *Sister Outsider: Essays and Speeches,* The Crossing Press. 1984.

10 Dennis Altman, 'Fear and loathing', *New Internationalist,* November 1989.

11 Vanessa Baird, *No-Nonsense Guide to Sexual Diversity,* Verso/NI. 2001.

12 Michelangelo Signorile, www.gay.com.

13 C Barillas, www.datalounge.com.

14 *Ibid.*

15 Amnesty International press release, 1 June 2004.

16 Martin Bauml Duberman, Martha Vicinus, George Chauncey eds, *Hidden from History,* Penguin. 1991.

17 Barry D Adam, Jan Willem Duyvendak, Andre Krouel eds, *The Global Emergence of Gay and Lesbian Politics,* Temple University Press. 1999.

18 Family Research Council, www.frc.org.

19 Jeffrey Weeks, 'Sexual Politics', *New Internationalist,* November 1989.

20 Judith Reisman, www.ifas.org.

I

1 Zachary I Nafaf, 'Whatever I feel', *New Internationalist,* April 1998.

2 *Ibid.*

3 *Ibid.*

4 Althaea Yronwode, 'Intersex Individuals dispute wisdom of surgery on infants', www.luckymojo.com appeared in 11 March 1999 issue of *Synapse,* campus newspaper of University of California at San Francisco Medical School.

5 ILGA world survey, joint press release ISNA/IGLHRC/NCLR, 26 October 1999.

6 'Outsouth: Sexual minorities in the majority world', *New Internationalist,* October 2000.

7 Zachary I Nafaf, *op cit.*

J

1 International Lesbian and Gay Association, *World Legal Survey update,* July 2002.

2 Amnesty International UK LGBT Network, Campaign Egypt Update, 2 July 2002, www.ailgbt.co.uk.

3 Byrne Fone, *Homophobia*, Metropolitan. 2000.

4 International Lesbian and Gay Association, *op cit.*

5 Ian Sumner, Molengraft Institute for Private Law, Utrecht. Research for PhD thesis collected from Swiss Institute for Comparative Law, Lausanne. May 2003.

6 Amnesty International, *Crimes of hate, conspiracy of silence*, AI Publications. 2001.

7 Amnesty International, Action Alert, 4 January 2002.

8 Ian Sumner, *op cit.*

9 *Ibid.*

10 *Salguerio Da Silva Mouta v Portugal*, Case number 33290/96, decided 21 December 1999 (judgement in French only).

11 Amnesty International USA, *Outfront*, www.amnestyusa.org.

12 *Gay Law News*, July-September 2003, www.gaylawnet.com.

13 CNN, 26 June 2003.

14 Judith Mackay, *The Penguin Atlas of Human Sexual Behavior*, Penguin US. 2000.

15 *Ibid.*

K

1 Quintin Crisp, *The Naked Civil Servant*, Jonathan Cape. 1968.

2 Rictor Norton, *The Myth of the Modern Homosexual*, Cassell. 1997.

3 *Ibid.*

L

1 Ashwini Sukthanker ed, *Facing the Mirror: Lesbian Writing from India*, Penguin India. 1999.

2 *The Trials of Oscar Wilde*: 1895, Uncovered Editions, The Stationery Office. 2001. Excerpts taken from transcripts of the trials conducted at the London Central Criminal Court, at the Old Bailey during April and May 1895.

3 Jeffrey Weeks, *Coming Out*, Quartet. 1977.

4 Wayne Dynes, *Encyclopedia of Homosexuality*, St James Press. 1990.

5 *Ibid.*

6 Lord Arran speaking in the House of Lords at the end of the debate on the Sexual Offences Act, 1967.

7 Ashwini Sukthanker, *op cit.*

M

1 Rex Wockner, *Great Gay Quotes*, www.geocities.com/WestHollywood/Heights/1734/great-gayquotes.html.

2 Evelyn Blackwood and Saskia Wieringa eds, *Female Desires*, Columbia University Press. 1999.

3 *Ibid.*

4 Ralf Michaels, *Same-sex Marriage: Canada, Europe and the United States*, Duke University School of Law, June 2003, and Partners Task Force for Gay and Lesbian

Couples – Legal Marriage Report, December 2002, www.buddybuddy.com.

5 Partners Task Force for Gay and Lesbian Couples – *Legal Marriage Report*, December 2002, www.buddybuddy.com.

6 'Brenda "weds" Sindi' by Sowetan, *Sunday World*, 1 December 2002, www.mask.org.za.

N

1 The Namibian, 23 April 2001, www.mask.org.za.

2 Poliyana Mangwiro interviewed by Vanessa Baird in 'Taboo breakers', *New Internationalist*, October 2000.

3 Mark Gevisser, 'Mandela's Stepchildren' in Peter Drucker ed, *Different Rainbows*, Gay Men's Press. 2000.

4 *Ibid.*

5 Randy P Conner, David Hatfield Sparks, Mariya Sparks, *Cassell's Encyclopedia of Queer Myth, Symbols and Spirit*, Cassell. 1997.

6 Shuaib Rahim, 'Out in Africa', *New Internationalist*, October 2000.

7 Ashwini Sukthanker, 'For people like us', *New Internationalist*, October 2000.

8 Vanessa Baird, *The No-Nonsense Guide to Sexual Diversity*, Verso/NI, 2001.

9 Anissa Helie, 'Holy hatred', *New Internationalist*, October 2000.

10 Raza Griffiths, 'Out and Muslim in the United Kingdom', *Pink Paper*, London, September 1999.

O

1 National Coalition for Gay, Lesbian, Bisexual and Transgendered Youth, www.outproud.org.

2 Elizabeth Wilson, *Mirror Writing*, Virago. 1992.

3 National Coalition for Gay, Lesbian, Bisexual and Transgendered Youth, op cit.

4 *Ibid.*

5 Rex Wockner, *Great Gay Quotes*, www.geocities.com/WestHollywood/Heights/1734/great-gayquotes.html.

6 *Ibid.*

7 Evelyn Blackwood and Saskia Wieringa eds, *Female Desires*, Columbia University Press. 1999.

P

1 Alexander Irwin, Joyce Millen and Dorothy Fallows, *Global Aids: Myths and Facts*, South End Press. 2003.

2 Chris McGreal, the *Guardian*, 29 July 2002/Behind the Mask News, www.mask.org.za.

3 International Gay and Lesbian Human Rights Association, Action Alert, 12 February 2003, www.iglhrc.org.

4 Human Rights Watch, 'State sponsored homophobia in South Africa', 2003.

5 Dennis Altman, 'The Emergence of a Non-government Response to AIDS', in Peter M Nardi and Beth E Schneider eds, *Social Perspectives in Lesbian and Gay*

Studies, Routledge, 1998.

6 Saleem Kidwai, 'Aliens in Lucknow', *New Internationalist,* June 2002, and IGLHRC, www.iglhrc.org.

7 Amnesty International, 2001.

8 Jeremy Seabrook, 'It's what you do', *New Internationalist,* October 2000.

9 UNAIDS, 'AIDS Epidemic Update', 2001.

10 *Ibid.*

11 Kate More and Stephen Whittle, *Reclaiming Genders,* Cassell. 1999.

12 'How to crush AIDS', *New Internationalist,* June 2002.

13 *Ibid.*

14 Gideon Mendel, 'Looking Aids in the face', the *Guardian,* 14 December 2002.

15 IGLHRC press release, 'People with AIDS Overpower Big Pharma in Thai Court', 9 October 2002.

Q

1 Rictor Norton, *The Myth of the Modern Homosexual,* Cassell, 1997.

2 Cherry Smith, *Lesbians Talk Queer Notions,* Scarlet Press. 1992.

3 *Ibid.*

4 *Ibid.*

5 *Ibid.*

6 Peter M Nardi and Beth E Schneider eds, *Social Perspectives in Lesbian and Gay Studies,* Routledge, 1998.

R

1 Lyrics by E Y Harburg.

2 Randy P Conner, David Hatfield Sparks and Mariya Sparks, *Cassell's Encyclopedia of Queer Myth, Symbol and Spirit,* Cassell, London and New York. Reprinted 1998.

3 Paul Zomcheck, 'Vexed by Rainbows', *Bay Area Reporter,* 26 June 1986; The Alyson Almanac, 'Rainbow Flag', 1989; Parade 90: San Francisco Gay/Lesbian Freedom Day Parade and Celebration, 'The Rainbow Flag', 24 June 1990.

S

1 Leslie Feinberg, *Trans Liberation,* Beacon Press. 1998.

2 *Ibid.*

3 Joan Nestle, *A Restricted Country,* Sheba. 1988.

4 Martin Bauml Duberman, Martha Vicinus, George Chauncey eds, *Hidden from History.* Penguin 1991.

5 Barry D Adam, Jan Willem Duyvendak and André Krouwel eds, *The Global Emergence of Lesbian and Gay Politics,* Temple University Press, Philadelphia. 1999.

T

1 International Gay and Lesbian Human Rights Commission website, www.iglhrc.org.

2 Amnesty International Canada, 'Argentina: It's time for justice', 22 June 2001.

3 Human Rights Watch Report 2002, www.hrw.org/lgbt.

4 Rex Wockner, *Windy City Times,* 1 january 2003.

5 International Gay and Lesbian Human Rights Commission website.

6 Amnesty International, *Crimes of hate, conspiracy of silence,* AI Publications. 2001.

7 Judith Mackay, *The Penguin Atlas of Human Sexual Behavior,* Penguin US. 2000.

8 Leslie Feinberg, *Trans Liberation,* Beacon Press. 1998.

9 Gilbert Herdt ed, *Third Sex, Third Gender,* Zone Books NY, 1994.

10 Leslie Feinberg, *op cit.*

11 Zachary I Nafaf, 'Whatever I feel', *New Internationalist,* April 1998.

12 Leslie Feinberg, *op cit.*

13 National Coalition for Gay, Lesbian, Bisexual and Transgendered Youth www.outproud.org.

U

1 Martin Bauml Duberman, Martha Vicinus, George Chauncey eds, *Hidden from History,* Penguin 1991.

2 Heinz Heger, *The Men with the Pink Triangle,* Gay Men's Press, 1972.

3 *Ibid.*

4 Eugen Kogon, *The Theory and Practice of Hell,* New York. 1950.

5 Heinz Heger, *op cit.*

6 Daniel Borillo, *L'Homophobie,* Presse Universitaire de France. June 2000.

7 Margrete Aarmo, 'How homosexuality became "un-African"', in Evelyn Blackwood and Saskia Wieringa eds, *Female Desires,* Columbia University Press. 1999.

8 Vanessa Baird, 'Out South – Sexual Minorities in the Majority World', *New Internationalist,* October 2000.

9 Resopnse to GenderDoc-M, following concern about homophobic comments made by Party Vice-President Vlad Cubreacov (Rex Wockner).

V

1 Martin Bauml Duberman, Martha Vicinus, George Chauncey eds, *Hidden from History,* Penguin 1991.

2 *Ibid* and Evelyn Blackwood and Saskia Wieringa eds, *Female Desires,* Columbia University Press. 1999.

3 Martin Bauml Duberman, Martha Vicinus, George Chauncey, *op cit.*

4 Byrne Fone, *Homophobia,* Metropolitan Books, New York. 2000.

5 *Ibid.*

6 Walter W Williams, *The Spirit and the Flesh,* Beacon

146

Press. 1986.

7 Anissa Helie, 'Holy Hatred' New Internationalist, October 2000 and Martin Bauml Duberman, Martha Vicinus, George Chauncey, *op cit.*

8 Martin Bauml Duberman, Martha Vicinus, George Chauncey, *op cit.*

9 Lotte van de Pol and Rudolf Dekker, *The Tradition of Transvesticism in Early Modern Europe*, Macmillan Press. 1989.

10 Robert Aldrich and Garry Wotherspoon eds, *Who's Who in Gay and Lesbian History*, Routledge, 2001.

11 Randy P Conner, David Hatfield Sparks and Mariya Sparks, *Cassell's Encyclopedia of Queer Myth, Symbol and Spirit*, Cassell, London and New York. 1997.

W

1 Lynne Harne and Rights of Women, *Valued Families,* The Women's Press. 1997.

2 Sol Kelly Jones, *Family Pride Colaition,* www.family-pride.org.

3 Evelyn Blackwood and Saskia Wieringa eds, *Female Desires*, Columbia University Press. 1999.

4 Amnesty International, *Crimes of hate, conspiracy of silence,* AI Publications. 2001.

5 Chou Wah-shan, 'Individual strategies of tongzhi empowerment in China', in Peter Drucker ed, *Different Rainbows*, Gay Men's Press. 2000.

6 Lynne Harne and Rights of Women, *op cit.*

7 Kate Mariat, 'Bygone illusions and begotten contradictions', in Jenny Morris ed, Alone Together, The Women's Press. 1992.

8 Lynne Harne and Rights of Women, *op cit.*

X

1 Kate Bornstein, *Gender Outlaw: On Men, Women and the Rest of Us,* Routledge. 1994.

2 Zachary I Nataf, 'Whatever I feel', *New Internationalist,* April 1998.

3 *Ibid.*

4 Jan Morris, Conundrum: *An extraordinary narrative of transsexualism,* Harcourt Brace Jovanovich. 1974.

5 Walter W Williams, *The Spirit and the Flesh,* Beacon Press. 1986.

6 Lou Sullivan, quoted in Zachary I Nataf, *Lesbians Talk Transgender,* Scarlet Press. 1996.

Y

1 Washington Post and http://home.mindspring.com/-derekhenkle/.

2 Diana Souhami, *The Trials of Radclyffe Hall,* Virago. 1999.

3 Response to GenderDoc-M (Rex Wockner).

4 Frontline: Assault on Gay America Interviews: Derek Henkle: http://www.pbs.org/wgbh/pages/frontline/shows/assault/interviews/henkle.html.

5 Interview by the National Lesbian and Gay Task Force, 2000.

6 Tina Machida, 'Sisters of Mercy' in Monika Reinfelder ed, *Amazon to Zami,* Cassell. 1996.

7 International Tribunal on Human Rights Violations Against Sexual Minorities, October 1999. www.iglhrc.org

8 Washington Post and http://home.mindspring.com/-derekhenkle/.

9 Supreme Court of Colombia, Pablo Enrique Torres Gutierrez and José Prieto Restrepo v Instituto Ginebra La Salle T-147493, judgement of 24 March 1998.

10 Frontline: Assault on Gay America Interviews: Derek Henkle: http://www.pbs.org/wgbh/pages/frontline/shows/assault/interviews/henkle.html.

Z

1 EZLN, *La Jornada,* 27 June 1999.

2 John Ross, 'Gay Purge in Mexico', NOW On/Newsfront/News 14-20 September 2000 www.now-toronto.com.

3 EZLN, *La Jornada,* 27 June 1999.

Further reading:

Aimée and Jaguar: a love story, Berlin 1943, by Erica Fischer, Bloomsbury, 1996.

Crimes of hate, conspiracy of silence, Amnesty International, 2001.

Different Rainbows, edited by Peter Drucker, Gay Men's Press, 2000.

Facing the Mirror: lesbian writing from India, edited by Ashwini Sukthankar, Penguin Books, 1999.

Global Sex, by Dennis Altman, University of Chicago Press, 2001.

Homophobia: a history, by Byrne Fone, Metropolitan Books, 2000.

The Mismeasure of Desire: The Science, Theory and Ethics of Sexual Orientation, by Edward Stein, Oxford, 1999.

Tipping the Velvet, by Sarah Waters, Virago, 1998.

Trans Liberation: beyond the pink or blue, by Leslie Feinberg, Beacon Press, 1998.

Trumpet, by Jackie Kay, Picador, 1998.

Who's Who in Gay and Lesbian History, edited by Robert Aldrich and Garry Wotherspoon, Routledge 2001.

Love in a Different Climate, by Jeremy Seabrook, Verso, 1999

Love speaks its name: gay and lesbian love poems, selected by JD McClatchy, Everyman's Library Pocket Series, 2001

Words like Weeds, Book One, by Anya Weinstein, iUniverse, 2003

Index

'To persecute people for their sexual orientation is to violate their fundamental human rights. All over the world lesbian, gay, bisexual and transgender people defend their right to be who they are, often at the risk of their lives. That is why those who care about human rights are doing something about it.'
– Linda Wilkinson, chair, Amnesty International UK

Amnesty International

Amnesty International is a worldwide movement of people campaigning for fundamental human rights. It has more than 1.8 million members, supporters and subscribers in over 150 countries around the world.

Amnesty International's vision is of a world in which every person enjoys the human rights enshrined in the Universal Declaration of Human Rights and other human rights standards.

Amnesty International's mission is to undertake research and action focused on preventing and ending grave abuses of the rights to physical and mental integrity, freedom of conscience and expression, and freedom from discrimination, within the context of its work to promote human rights.

Amnesty International believes that persecuting a person for their sexual orientation is a violation of fundamental human rights. The organisation campaigns for the release of anyone imprisoned solely on the grounds of homosexuality and supports LGBT people who are under threat for defending their rights.

www.amnesty.org.uk
www.ai-lgbt.org
www.ailgbt.co.uk